PARENT

TO

PARENT

A Personal Journey of Raising Extraordinary Children
by Teaching Essential Life Skills

B. JANINE FULLA

 FriesenPress

Suite 300 - 990 Fort St
Victoria, BC, V8V 3K2
Canada

www.friesenpress.com

ISBN
978-1-5255-1117-2 (Hardcover)
978-1-5255-1118-9 (Paperback)
978-1-5255-1119-6 (eBook)

1. FAMILY & RELATIONSHIPS, PARENTING, CHILD REARING

Distributed to the trade by The Ingram Book Company

What people are saying about "Parent to Parent"

"Wow! I love this book. Jan captures and shares lessons for the soul, for every child and parent. There are many parenting books about babies' cries and toddlers' tantrums, but this book is different. It addresses the most important and elusive aspect of our lives, 'the soul.' 'We learn to parent every day,' Jan says, and she's right. Jan takes us on her own journey through childhood, sharing her history and how it has empowered her and her children. This book helps us to stop and breathe, realizing we are in this together with our kids."

"By nourishing our children's souls and our own, we give and receive an enduring and invaluable gift; raising and becoming good citizens, good people. Jan writes about qualities that nourish the soul, things like self esteem, gratitude, gut instinct, volunteering and giving. Jan reminds us what really matters in life; loving, laughing, making memories and making sense of life."

"I believe '*Parent to Parent*' is helpful to all, from new parents to those of us whose children are grown. This book is an invaluable guide along the challenging, sometimes confusing, but always rewarding journey known as parenthood."

"I am looking forward to more guidance from Jan, and am thankful she has reminded me of all that I hold so dear."

Patty Mack
LifeStylewithPattyMack.com

"From the opening quote to the final page, I appreciated this book so much. It was like sitting down with a cup of tea with Jan right across from me sharing her wisdom. I highly recommend this book for everyone who has children in their life. While my own son is grown up, some things that I read gave me pause to think of how I respond to my three sweet grandchildren."

"Thank you for putting this work out into the world."

Carolyne Taylor, Community Leader
Carolynetaylor.com

"What a great book! Jan has accomplished a very accessible guide for parents to tackle the most important work in their lives, raising competent, thoughtful people. Jan has created a wonderful guide illustrating parenting advice through engaging stories of her own experience with her children. Parents can relate to this book as Jan shares not only her parenting successes, but her failures as well. Most importantly, the lessons learned from these failures and how to make the next time better. Jan encourages parents to listen to their children, so that they can find out more about them. Too often we as parents, think we know everything there is to know about our child."

"Educators would love parents to read this book, so that they can have meaningful conversations with parents about their children."

Jim Cambridge,
Superintendent, School District #62

"As a Preschool Teacher with over 30 years experience, and a parent myself, I recommend 'Parent to Parent' as a go to guide for parents or teachers. This is a 'no fluff' book about not being the so called perfect parent, but about being the best you can be. There are times while raising our children that we can feel alone, this book will remind you that you are not alone. As Jan writes, parenting is not a popularity contest or about giving in to your child's wants, and she gives us some examples on how to do this better."

'Take *Parent to Parent* with you on your journey and enjoy."

Patricia Barbon
Rainbows and Dreams Preschool

"In a world where common sense is no longer common, comes along an uncomplicated little book full of wise words and practical advice. It is meant for every parent, no matter your own personal upbringing or present family status, who wants to become better at parenting and raise exceptional human beings. It won't take you long to figure out that Janine Fulla has done more than write a handbook on good parenting skills. What she has really done is written a 'common sense' guide to remind us all how to be exceptional human beings."

"A must give, thoughtful gift for every new parent you know."

Diana Frajman
Croneconfidence.com

"Jan has written a unique book, a one of a kind parenting guide. Beautifully written and inspiring. Jan has documented her sincere journey through parenthood. By sharing not only her insights, and personal experiences with her own children, she has created this generations 'go-to' manual which contains priceless content for our 'parenting toolbox.' Her take on love, wisdom and patience can help us all raise authentic children, while crushing their limiting beliefs."

"The proof in '*Parent to Parent*' is in her own children. Kailee and Brenden are both self-empowered, authentic, brave, kind and out to make our world a better place to be."

"Jan's book inspires us to not only be better parents but, better people. An absolute must read that will be a life changer for many!"

"I've spent countless hours helping people sort through parenting issues and issues with their parents. This book will help both. It graciously acknowledges the inherent challenges of parenting while identifying the essential parenting principles that lead to healthy hearts and homes."

CONTENTS

DEDICATION

To My Children,
"If I had to choose between breathing or loving you,
I would say 'I Love You' with my last breath"
—Shannon Dermott

This book is dedicated to my children, Kailee and Brenden, for without their belief in me, this book would not have been written.

Without hesitation, they encouraged, supported and cheered me on. They have been and are, my accountability coaches. They wanted this book out in the world to help other parents and children come together. Thank you from deep in my heart for all the long phone calls, the discussions of this book, the reading and re-reading and mostly for your unending support and love.

There is simply no stronger or deeper bond that I have in my life than the relationship I have with my children. They have touched my soul immensely, and have brought nothing but joy, happiness and light to my world. I admire them, adore them and am eternally grateful and honoured to call them my children, and share this very special relationship.

"I Love you both more than you can ever know or imagine … and
I will Love you with all my heart and soul, till the end of time…"
"You Have Made my Life Beautiful …"

~ And for those who are close to me… and you know who you are…I am blessed by your encouragement, support, and patience during the writing of this book. To you, I am grateful and blessed beyond measure…

~My love to you always…

I posed a question to my kids who are now in their mid-twenties, asking them why they wanted me to write this book. Here are their unedited responses:

From my Son~

"Why did I encourage my mom to write this book? I wanted her to write this book because I know it has the power to change your life. Change your life by saving the most important relationship in the world, a parent to a child. She will open your eyes and inspire you to become the best you, and the best parent you can be. She inspires me every time I see her with her positivity, strength and class. I would not have wanted to be raised any other way."

"I look forward to the future when I have kids and this book will be there to help guide me to have the same relationship as we do. If you do not have kids or your kids have already grown up, don't worry you still will be able to take things from this book. These are just some reasons why I wanted her to write this."

"Enjoy! Love you, Mom!"

From my Daughter~

"Why did I want Mom to write this book? In life, there are few people that have the ability to light up a room and share insightful and profound stories. One of those people I am fortunate to call my mom. Everything that has happened in her life

– from being adopted, to the relationship she has with parents, to her divorce, to raising her children – has led her with the tools and strength to write this book."

"The relationship you have with your child is a relationship you will have forever. No matter what stage you are at as a parent there is room for growth and this book will encourage you to test that. It is never too late to establish a loving, respectful, exciting, and empowering relationship with your children. I have that relationship with the woman that has written this book and I am so grateful for that. So, for the hundred times you have told me that you have been proud of me, here it is back to you."

"Mom, I am so incredibly proud of you. I love you!"

FOREWARD

"Coming together is a beginning.
Keeping together is progress.
Working together is success."
—Henry Ford

Welcome to the Team!!

From the moment your child is born, until the day they leave your home to start their own life, you will be their personal coach, and… your children are in training.

You will teach them skills, have practices, repeat the drills, repeat the drills, (yes, I did say that twice) teach them how to work together with the rest of the team… ('team' being… the world), and how to make good choices in their efforts to win the game of life. As a coach, you will also teach them how to feel good even if they missed the pass, to be grateful for the opportunity to be here to learn, and when they can't go any further on your team, they will be ready and have the necessary tools to start their own… life team.

Along with being their coach, you will be astounded at the amount of roles you will need to play. You will require hats for the following positions: Nurse, Referee, Taxi Driver, Bus Driver, Policeman, Fireman, Psychologist, Pastor, Teacher, Nurturer, Short Order Cook, Cleaner, Camp Leader, Supervisor,

Life Guard, Banker, Nutritionist, Lie Detector, Counsellor, Chaperone, Confident and so many, many more.

It's OK... Breathe... You've Got This!!!

So many people who are parents of older children, will tell parents of younger children, "Enjoy every moment, the time passes too quickly." I remember being told this so many times by the generation before me that I dreaded it. In my head I would think, "actually, things are moving at a very slow pace, thank you," and never had the nerve to say it out loud. It felt that way to me, with the exception of the first year, when they seem to change daily and go from sleeping all the time to actually eating real food, walking and sometimes running. So much progress in such a short time!

The challenging two's and three's really seemed to go on far longer than we all needed it to, and then when the kids were six and eight until they were twelve and fourteen, well... it really seemed to be an eternity. Then it happened, quite suddenly just like the generation before said it would. They went from a toddler to asking for the keys to my car in what seemed like maybe... a week! How could this happen so fast? Funny we never want to believe the generation before, we figure we know more and we know it better and then... it turns out... sometimes we don't.

I became grateful for the generation before with their simple reminders to cherish every moment... could it be because I am now in the category of 'the generation before' and I know this because, now that my children are adults, I hear myself saying to the new mom's of the world, the exact same thing... and they look at me the exact same way...

INTRODUCTION

"Your children will see what you're all about by what you live,
Rather than what you say"
—Wayne Dyer

This book is from a Parent to a Parent. I am not a counsellor or psychiatrist; I do not have any degrees or letters after my name. I can guarantee at one point or another on the journey of raising your children, you will feel like you should have at least one degree but, I can assure you it will not be necessary. I have my parenting experience, many years of facilitating parenting groups and some personal awakenings to share with you, that may help your parenting experience.

This book is about the emotional health of your children and not about rules regarding bedtimes, napping or what to feed your child. Your child will present different circumstances to you throughout their growing years and this book is about how to deal with those situations using wisdom and patience and provide you with information on how to empower and uplift your child. It is about developing their character through life lessons, and mostly about you, the parent.

I am amazed at the statistics I read in the news about children, and in particular teens between the ages of 15–17 who suffer from low self-esteem. Why are these children suffering?

Is it social media? It likely has something to do with it, however many children have been left behind in the adult's pursuit of prosperity, and as a result children are not given what they need in terms of developing their character, confidence, and flounder when looking for what makes them authentic. Why is the 'home' consisting of beautiful things and big screen TV's and expressing our pride in these 'things' when the 'home' is somewhere our children should be finding their inner self, given the freedom to express themselves and mature their nature without ridicule, which should come with more pride from the parents than their accumulations. I am not saying that you cannot enjoy what you work so hard for, I am only suggesting that you appreciate your children more than your things.

Having children is not an accessory and yet many parents treat children as such. Once the accessory starts to have a mind of its own, parents get scared and believe they need to make rules and more rules and become controlling. They will say 'no' more often than not, to define the child/parent roles and hierarchy and think it constitutes being a good parent. Children are seen as inconvenient to their own pursuit and put the children aside without much contemplation. Later, when the children are teenagers and the parents are having issues, rather than the parent looking at what created these issues, they casually move the children aside and the child's behaviour is explained as 'it's just who they are.'

This book is about how to *not* push your children aside because you don't know what to do with them. This book is intended to make you think about your parenting options and parenting plans. My goal for this book is to inspire you to be the best parent you can be.

> *"Let's raise children who won't have to recover from their childhood."* —Pam Leo

Many times in our life we make choices for self-improvement, and being a good parent is a choice. By you reading this book, you are making a choice to be the best parent you can be. It is a big step, and a big commitment, and I applaud you.

I have used many examples in this book of real life situations that have come up while raising my children. The reason I have included these examples is for you to insert your own circumstances in the scenarios and rather than having a reactionary response to the circumstances, I am inviting you to pause for thought as to how you are going to handle these different situations. Many of these examples come from my personal experience with my children, other examples are from my experience in facilitating a parent group for parents that were wanting to have better relationships with their teenage children. Many of the parents that attended my group have asked me to write down my methods so they would have a reference, and my children have asked the same of me.

Growing Years

"It takes courage to grow up,
And become who you really are."
—e.e. cummings

I am very proud that my parents have been married for over 60 years as this is so rare these days. My relationship with my parents has had its ups and downs just as many parent/child relationships have. At times, I have had a wonderful relationship with my parents and at other times I felt as though I never really 'fit in.' I always knew my parents loved me but I also had the feeling I never really pleased them. I have no doubt they did the best they could, and I am aware that other life events were taking place in their world that perhaps prevented us from bonding the way I would have liked. I don't doubt I caused them strife as I floundered through my teen years and was grounded more times than I can count.

I always carried a sadness that I didn't have a close emotional relationship with my parents, one that I felt I could be free with my personal expression of who I am. I do love my parents even though our relationship has not always been entirely tranquil.

I decided I wanted to have a different relationship with my children, I wanted the deep conversations, the laughter and the memories. I wanted this so much that I was prepared to make whatever sacrifices necessary to ensure they had everything in our relationship that I had always longed for.

——————— Awakening to a New Life ———————

"Co-Parenting.
It's not a competition between two homes.
It's a collaboration of parents doing
what is best for the kids."
—Heather Hetchler

I was married to my children's father for ten years and had my daughter when I was twenty-seven and my son when I was twenty-nine.

When my kids were just six and four, I was thrown a curve ball, one that rocked my world. Their father and I divorced. This was not in my life plan and now I had two young children, and shared custody. It was no longer raising my children in one 'stable home,' but two homes for my kids and two different rules and teachings. Not only were the rules and teachings different, so were our circumstances financially. On top of that, neither their father nor I came from a broken family and so this was new to both of us.

I do want to point out that their father was and is, a very good man, kind and humorous, generous and determined. We divorced because of very personal reasons, none of which are relevant to this book. All that matters is that we were divorced with two small children. We remained friendly, putting our personal feelings aside and focused on raising our children, and we both agreed to put our children first and foremost. Yes, we occasionally stumbled and emotions took over from time to time however, for the most part we did our best at co-parenting.

So, realizing this is very new territory for me as my children's upbringing was not to be in one home as I had, and I had no idea how it felt to be in a broken home, my challenge seemed larger than I could handle.

> *"You must first teach a child he is loved. Only then is he ready to learn everything else."*
> —Amanda Morgan

My goal for this book is to inspire you. I want you to know that no matter what your family circumstances are at this moment: single parent, divorced, married, or any other denomination of family, or the circumstances that you were brought up in, you have the ability to parent well. No longer do we need to use the excuses that we had a difficult childhood and cannot do better ... we do better, when we know better.

If you are a single parent reading this, please don't be discouraged by the people who say children from single parent homes do not turn out well. I was told this by a number of people when I was newly divorced and my response to them was, 'Just Watch Me!' You have the power in yourself to raise great, happy, authentic children, it just takes a commitment and awareness.

Believe in yourself...

I do know that I did the very best I could do in each moment of raising my children, without fail. I was committed and they always received my best and yes, some moments were better than others. This is not about perfection, it is about doing your best.

There was a day I had a realization that altered my parenting and made me realize just how important raising a child truly is. This moment formed me and taught me that I can be bigger than my circumstances and I have the power to do this job of raising great people.

––––––– My Children are My Forever –––––––

"Children are our greatest treasure.
They are our future."
—Nelson Mandela

This realization made me look at a bigger picture. Take a moment and look at life, and what comes, and what goes. When I looked over my life and the lives of others, a common denominator existed: friends had come and gone, pets had come and gone, even husbands and wives come and go, along with other things like jobs, cars and homes. The one thing in my life that will never change no matter what is … I will always be the mother of these two beautiful children … nothing can change that. This makes my children my 'forever.'

This was such a profound realization for me, as someone who is forever in your life deserves your full attention. Your children deserve the best of you and nothing less. What you put into this responsibility and relationship is exactly what your children will get out of it. It is an incredible responsibility and a privilege. Remember this every day.

One day, my son at the age of seventeen sat with me and told me he was beyond happy, so much was happening in his world and he was excited about life! He said to me then, words I will never forget, "Mom, I want you to be around when one day I have kids of my own. I want you to help me to raise them as you have raised us because… I Love My Life!"

> *"Be somebody for your kids to look up to."*
> —Webbie

Apparently, under the circumstances of being a divorced single parent, I did something right to have the honour of hearing these words from him. Now, I want more parents to hear these words from their children. I want this to happen to you.

In that special moment of my son expressing those words, a quick reflection of the years of raising my children went through my mind. Times of talking for hours about their problems, times of picking them up from friends' late at night, shuffling off to soccer practice and dance lessons and at times what seemed like an army of kids sleeping over, feeding them all, and times of being frustrated as a parent, feeling tired and picking myself up anyway, and the stress of running a house and raising kids, alone. That moment made all of the less beautiful and inconvenient times of parenting so very worthwhile and worth every single second to hear those words from my son. There is no greater feeling than knowing your children are happy … within.

My children are now adults and I could not be more proud of the people they have turned out to be. They are authentic, confident, inspiring, supportive, and still make me laugh every day. They are my joy, and we share a bond and a union that is unconditional and our relationship is open and trusted to this day.

It warms my heart that one day when I have grandchildren, they will be brought up in a similar way, and that the generation beyond will do an even better job at raising their children. Our children are the future and this is our contribution to the world… that is pretty magnificent stuff! Empower yourself and your children, make a choice and a decision and a commitment. This is your forever and your legacy…

Be Aware… Be Conscious… Get Excited… and Get Ready for the Most Profound Journey of Your Life …

UNDERSTANDING YOURSELF FIRST

"Your history does not dictate your future."
—Leigh Ann Napier

Looking at ourselves first is the most important step in raising our children. Our children are new to this world, ready to learn what we teach them and as young children, they have yet to develop any filters. As parents, we have filters through which we view life based on our life experiences. If you look at your child and wonder where they learned their behaviour from, it is likely from the parents and at times, it can be hard to accept responsibility. We must take responsibility.

I would like you to consider these next few points and remember them throughout this book.

- "You Cannot Give Away Something You Do Not Have"
  - If you do not have patience, you cannot give patience
  - If you do not have compassion for others, you cannot give compassion

- "You Cannot Teach Something You Cannot Do Yourself"
  - You cannot teach your child not to yell if you are yelling
  - You cannot teach your child to be honest if you are not honest
- "You Cannot Ask Your Child To Do Something You Wouldn't Do"
  - You cannot ask your child to spend less time on social media if you spend just as much time on it as them

This is a new day to raise children, it is the era of the Internet and lost conversations, games online and not outdoors. The parent now has new competition with electronics and not just the influence of the naughty little child down the street. Because of this, it makes the parenting role even more crucial than years gone by. It is time for the parent to step in and be present, teach life skills to your child and not leave it up to society, teachers and/or social media... believe me, social media can destroy your child's emotional growth while at the same time being entertaining.

—— Unfinished Emotional Business? ——

*"Nothing has any power over me
other than that which I give it
through my conscious thoughts."*
—Tony Robbins

One of the hardest things to do is to look at ourselves objectively. Sometimes it hurts and we don't want to look, sometimes it can make us shake our heads and sometimes we just laugh. The important part of looking at ourselves when we are raising children is to identify if there is any unfinished emotional business within ourselves.

Another way of looking at it is, is there anything emotionally in you that stops you from going forward in the direction you want to go, what is holding you back? Is there stuff from your past that should have been boxed up years ago and left at the curb? Don't ignore that stuff or be embarrassed about it. Everyone has had it. If you cannot recognize your own stuff, try asking yourself a few questions. Do you have tapes that keep playing in your mind that perhaps make you feel not good enough, smart enough, funny enough, rich enough, brave enough, anything that stops you from believing you are enough? Guess what… *You Are Enough!*

> *"Can you remember who you were before the world told you who you should be?"*
> —Danielle LaPorte

If you have any of these beliefs, ask yourself where did they show up in your life and how have they controlled you. Did any of them come from your childhood? Were you missing anything from your childhood and what would you wish for if you could go back to that time? If you had the childhood you wished you could have had, how would your life be different now?

If these limiting self-beliefs are holding you back in your life, the best advice I can give you is to find someone to help you through this. If it is a trusted friend or a therapist it is worth the time and expense because you will then be free to be who you were meant to be.

> *"Rather than being your thoughts and emotions, be the awareness behind them."*
> —Eckhart Tolle

We cannot go back in time and change anything. We have what we have and our emotional self is what it is. The good news is, we still have the power of choice, to choose to make a better beginning for our children. The lack of what we needed when we were children has shaped our life and our life's perspectives. Limiting self-beliefs are not healthy for us, and all they deserve from us is the big heave-ho! Understand, with the dedication to work through tough moments and/or memories, you no longer need to feel like a victim of your childhood. Imagine the difference in your life when you change how you see yourself and start realizing your amazing abilities. All it takes is a decision, a decision that you will not allow the rest of your life to be guided by these ridiculous negative beliefs about yourself. You are limitless… you are all you need to be, and… *love yourself…*

—— The Meaning of Making a Decision ——

"Sometimes it's the smallest decision
That can change your life forever."
—Keri Russell

The time has come to make a decision to change those limited self beliefs that have perhaps gotten in your way. Now that you have or want a child, there is no better time or reason for dealing with some personal issues. This is one of the biggest gifts you can give to your child...

It is human nature to try to do things the easy way, and how many of us have tried this method and it usually ends up with us saying, 'well... that would have turned out better if I put a bit more effort into it.' Short cuts are just that, and it leaves us short of achieving our goals and short of moving forward to where we want to be. Then, we are just full of wonderful excuses as to why we are not where we want to be. Making excuses is not the easy way. It is just as limiting as self limiting beliefs!

Personally, once I decided to become the best parent I could be, there was no turning back and the commitment was fully engaged. I did not say that I *would like* to be a great parent or I am *going to try* to be a great parent, as that is non-committal. A decision to do or be something means making a full commitment and cutting yourself off from any other possibility. Period.

For some, this may be a little scary as making a decision usually involves making a change. Without change, your limiting self beliefs have permission to continue to hold you back... until you *decide* otherwise. Change happens in a second, the second you decide. Your child is about to go through some significant changes from a new born to an adult and they don't have the opportunity to say, "gosh, I have to go through all those changes in a matter of eighteen years! I am afraid of change so I don't think I will participate and will just stay as I am, thanks." Can you imagine? If your child can boldly face all the changes they are about to embark on, how about you the parent, make a few changes of your own.

> *"We cannot control what emotions or circumstances we will experience next, but we can choose how we will respond to them."*
> —Gary Zukav

Each person, no matter their circumstances, is entitled to a peace of heart and happiness, it is your birthright. You are the only person in control of you and your emotions, thoughts, actions, choices and decisions, no one else. You have made it this far in life, and that makes you a survivor. That makes you brave. That makes you capable and worthwhile.

Now you want to raise a child. Do you want to give that child all the negative self-limiting beliefs that controlled you or held you back, and maybe even add some new ones, because raising a child will create more self-doubt, believe me! Or, do you want to give this little person, this little miracle the greatest chance and opportunity to be confident, self-assured and happy?

——— A Bit of Parental Homework ———

> *"When it is obvious that the goals cannot be reached,*
> *Don't adjust the goal,*
> *Adjust the action."*
> —Confucius

Spend some time with a piece of paper and a pen and write down the things you wished were different in your childhood or upbringing. For this exercise, it is not about your house not being big enough, being embarrassed about your parents' car, other kids having more money and things. I want you to write about the inside emotional stuff. This is your private list, you don't have to show anyone, only you, and please be truthful to yourself.

Some thoughtful questions to ask yourself could be ...
- Did you have enough praise?
- Were you able to talk openly about your feelings?
- Were you yelled at and belittled as a child?
- Did your parents find you capable or incapable?
- Were you called names by your family?
- Were they positive or negative?
- Were you ignored as a single child or forgotten because of many siblings?
- Was your sibling always doing right and you always doing wrong?
- Was it the other way around?
- Did your parents work all the time or, were they with you every second?
- Were you always being blamed?
- Did your parents abandon you?

Pay attention to how you feel when you answer these questions and ask some of your own questions. Did some of those questions make your insides go tight? Did some just do nothing to you because it wasn't your issue? Use this as a guideline. When our bodies react physically, that can be an indication that something is feeling true about this statement and perhaps it is an area to look at and work on. Focus on any of those questions for which you did experience a reaction, either physical or emotional. If left ignored there is a big chance that those feelings will be recycled again to your children, and they will bear the emotional scars without ever even understanding why. Without consideration, we can unintentionally put our own emotional pain and afflictions onto our children.

Life is full of ups and downs all meant for us to learn and grow and all experiences are different with different lessons. Let's consider looking at life as if it were a story, our own personal story where we are here to learn from these lessons and everyone here has certain lessons to learn. If we the parents do not learn our own lessons in life or deal with our own issues, they can be passed down to our children to deal with. Should our children deal with our issues? For example, if in our child's life story, they have ten issues or lessons to learn in their lifetime and then the parent drops their own ten issues or lessons on top of the child's list (because we haven't yet learned our own lessons), the child now has twenty lessons and issues to work through, and half of them were never meant for that child. The child now has way too much to learn and accomplish and is now overwhelmed with life, and the child and parents will have some large obstacles to overcome.

> *"Parenthood... It's about guiding the next generation, and forgiving the last."* —Peter Krause

This is where we pass down from generation to generation our own pain and suffering, because we refuse to look at our issues and deal with them. The parent then parents the way they were parented, maintaining the generational cycle and refusing the task of looking inward to see what needs to be fixed. Children should not have to deal with their parents' emotional health.

Many families suffer from the generational cycle. In some families this is more than acceptable and everyone is happy and well adjusted, baring in mind that... how many 'functional' families actually exist? Sometimes it is a good plan to look at the generations before yours, and ask questions about why.

This reminds me of a brief and enlightening story to help understand the generations and the importance of stepping back, to look forward. There are many different variations of the story and the author is unknown.

The Pot Roast Story

A newly wed husband noticed that every time his wife cooked a pot roast she would first cut an inch off either end before putting it in the oven. When he asked why, she said, "Because that's how you are suppose to cook pot roast." Unsatisfied with her answer he pushed until she admitted that she had learned it from her mother.

Waiting until a visit with his wife's mother, the husband asked, "Your daughter tells me you taught her to cook pot roast by first cutting an inch off each end?" To which the mother replied, "well of course, that's how pot roast is cooked." But the husband was not to be deterred, and after pressing his mother-in-law on the subject she finally admitted that she'd learned it from her mother.

This meant the husband had to ask the wife's grandmother. When he finally got his chance he asked, "Your daughter told me you taught her to cut an inch off each end of a pot roast before cooking. She swore it was a requirement, but I'm dying to know why? Is there any sane reason to throw away two inches of perfectly good meat in order to cook a pot roast?"

Laughing, the grandmother said, "Oh, heaven's no! You see in those days we were very poor and didn't own much cookware. I cut the ends off the pot roast so it would fit in my only pan!!"

And so ends the story...

— Children Need to be Their Own Person —

*"A lot of parents will do anything for their kids
except let them be themselves."*
—Banksy

Children are meant to be individuals, their own persons. They are not expected to have the same feelings as anyone else nor see life the same way as their parents. If you put two people in the same circumstance, each will feel it differently. Each person who has a life here, has their very own story. They are all meant to be as unique as each of our faces. Even twins have some differences and the differences should be embraced. Just because a grandchild does not want to run the family business does not make him or her wrong, only that they have a different life story and that is what their life's purpose is. Our part as a parent is to encourage their uniqueness and embrace who they are.

> *"Believe in your children, and they will believe in themselves, too."* —Vicki Reece

I always told my children to show me who they are, I want to learn all about you. It was magic to watch the show. While their true self emerged I learned so much about them, and they taught me so much about life. The secret is to be open to who they are and let go of our own expectations of who we think they should be.

You are on this journey with basically no map, no GPS, no guide on how to raise these children with the exception of how you were raised yourself. Parents generally have good intentions and sometimes just need a little help to move in the right direction.

I explained to my kids that I am a parent for the very first time and I don't have all the answers on how to do it right. I asked that they help me be the best parent I can be to them. I told them if they have an idea or thought that would make me better, or if they didn't agree with what I was doing, to talk to me about their thoughts. It didn't mean they would always get their way, it did mean they had an opinion and I was willing to listen to that. We are in this raising and growing up together, so why not work together.

In doing this, the children felt empowered, it taught them they have a voice, which is such a great lesson for later in life. They will grow confident in speaking out about what matters to them, both as a child and as an adult. I encourage you to give your children a voice. This also developed great communication between us as they knew without a doubt they could come to me and talk about anything that might be on their minds. Because of this, we had no yelling in my home, no fighting in my home as there was no reason to when we discussed everything and understood each other.

> *"Children are not casual guests in our home. They have been loaned to us temporarily for the purpose of loving them and instilling a foundation of values on which their future lives will be built."* —James Dobson

Just because you hold the title of 'Mom' or 'Dad' does not give you the right to treat your children poorly. You do not own your children, they are a temporary gift.

Faith is Your Friend

"Faith is like WiFi
It's invisible but it has the power to
Connect you to what you need."
—Drake Mariani

Don't worry, I will not get all preachy preachy with you but figured that while we are taking a closer look at who we are, it is worth a mention and I do wish for you to have an open mind on the subject. Many people I know have faith however the word "God" is too loaded for them and makes some uncomfortable. Not to worry, you can refer to Him in any way you like, The Force, The Divine, The Universe, The Spirit, Your Higher Power, The Super Power, The Grand Master... whatever it is that relates to you.

If you do not have a relationship with your Higher Power, I guarantee at one point or another you will wish that you did... even if you are dead set against it. You will find yourself saying quiet prayers to Him when your child has a cold as an infant and cannot breathe through their nose, asking for protection over your child while they venture off for the first time without you or when they take the car alone for the first time, and when you end up in the hospital because your child thought it was a good idea to wear a superman cape and try to fly off the sun deck. At times like this, God or your Higher Power will be called by you to help, and wouldn't it be great if you could just pray for your child instead of also praying at the same time for forgiveness, for all the years you doubted Him. He will be your best friend, I promise.

It is far more powerful to say a quiet prayer to someone you have a relationship with, than someone you don't.

—————— Managing your Anger Emotion ——————

"A moment of patience in a moment of anger prevents a thousand moments of regret."
—Ali Ibn Talib

It is important to have a plan, even a basic landscape at the very beginning of parenting. What you put out to your child is usually what you will receive. In understanding ourselves, we also need to understand our triggers for anger, and management of it. Perhaps you are the type that is slow to anger and once you reach the breaking point, everything explodes. Or perhaps you are the type that blows up often as a release and maybe anger is just not an issue for you. Whatever your reaction to anger is, understand your triggers and have a way to deal with it.

Maybe you need a quiet time to reflect, maybe you need to go to the gym. Whatever it is, know what it is because raising a child will push all your buttons at one time or another. If anger is a serious issue, then I ask you to get the help you need to manage it before you subject your newborn child to the outcome. There is nothing more frightening to a child than to see a parent angry and not understand where it came from or how it got there. Children will decide to take it on themselves and blame themselves for it. This again is not fair to a child as it is an adult problem.

> *"Stop making your child a victim of your anger."* —Unknown

At times anger can even show up in our energy. If we are upset about something, our own personal energy changes and children pick up on this more often than not. If nothing is said about this 'energy' or the elephant in the room so to speak, the child will automatically assume they did something wrong to create this feeling. I recommend that if there are some trying times going on in your adult world, it is always a good time to talk to your children to let them know there is an adult issue happening and that although Mom and/or Dad seem upset, it is because of the issue and not them.

Remember we do not have to be perfect, and letting them know that issues come up from time to time and you are working through them will benefit a child. When they have their own issues as teens, they will feel more comfortable coming to you and explaining that they have an issue and it is not anything to do with the parent. They learn quickly by watching and doing what the parent does, and this is a great way to develop good communication.

Take a Few Deep Breaths

"Pause for a moment
And reflect."
—Oprah & Deepak

In frustrating times, it can be easy to yell at your child for something very small just because the adult is dealing with their own emotions. Unfortunately, because it is our children that are with us most of the time, they are the ones receiving the fallout.

If this happens, I ask that you to take a few deep breaths and then sit the child down and apologize for your behaviour and that your yelling at them was misguided and not their fault. Clear this up as early as possible. Believe me, you do not want your child to be frightened of you. Once fear is part of the equation, the fear will stop your child from coming to you with something important, and perhaps it's something that should be discussed with you, the parent and not a friend of your child's. On the good side, by demonstrating this behaviour to your child, your child will learn how to handle such situations should they happen to them, either as a child or as an adult.

If you are asking yourself why would you apologize to your child… just put yourself in the child's shoes for a moment. See the situation from their perspective and… ask yourself 'why' again…

——— Parenting Good Days and ——— Parenting Bad Days

"Consistent Parenting…
I may not always know what my child will do,
but my child should ALWAYS know what I will do…"
—Unknown

Another consideration in understanding yourself for the purpose of parenting is, how do you parent when you are having a good day vs. when you are having a bad day? Similar to the universal question, 'who are you when no one is looking?'

It is truly ok to have bad days, we all do. Be aware of the different ways you handle your child on one of your good days and on one of your bad days. In being aware of yourself and your mood, I recommend trying to be as consistent as possible with your child. In my parenting group experiences, children were often caused to pause and sometimes suffer unnecessarily from not knowing if it was a good time or a bad time to approach their parent. This uncertainty can drive a child to make their own decisions to avoid any negative reaction, and chose to take the path of least resistance... (a common and normal behaviour for both parent and child). What happens next is the child begins to tell lies to the parent as they see this as a safer alternative. It is not the only reason a child will tell a lie but it is certainly one of them. After a while, the lie becomes habit.

When parents catch their child telling lies, the parent cannot understand why the child would do this, and only look at the child for answers. I encourage you the parent to look at what you may have done, or not done to accommodate this behaviour in your child. Parents, look at the environment you have created first and then ask yourself, if I were this child, would I feel safer telling a lie in this circumstance also? If so, do what is necessary to eliminate the fear of approaching you, from the child eyes.

—— Parents Do Not Have To Be Perfect ——

"There are no perfect parents, and there are no perfect children, but there are plenty of perfect moments along the way."
— Dave Willis

Remember parents don't have to be perfect. You are now in a position that gives you no days off, not even an hour off. You are in the most important job of your life, with no long weekends without responsibility, no overtime, no Mother/Father award at the end of the year. You will however, by working hard, paying attention and being conscious...

Receive the Largest Bonus of Your Life...
It Just Won't be Monetary...

WHAT THE SCHOOLS DON'T TEACH IS A PARENT'S MANDATE

"The difference between School and Life?
In School, you're taught a lesson and then given a test.
In Life, you're given a test that teaches you a lesson."
—Tom Bodett

How many parents think and believe that when your child goes to school, they will learn their academics, plus how to deal with life and will somehow figure out their place in this world?

Why wait until your child has an issue at school with being bullied, or wait until your child talks back to the teacher and the principal is calling you? Why wait until you learn that your child has no friends and is feeling depressed? Why wait until your child fails at something and does not know how to handle the rejection? Why wait? The truth is, some of the things your child goes through, those difficulties of growing up, may never even come to your attention, unless you are plugged in to them. So many children are left to try and figure out life themselves and that is not always a good plan.

Schools are meant to teach academics: spelling, reading, writing, math, sciences, English, and in some schools, French. They are not meant to teach your child the foundational values of life and how to make good choices nor lift their self-esteem.

— Find Out What Your Child is Good At —

"Follow your own passion,
Not your parents',
Not your teachers,
..Yours."
—Robert Ballard

When I was growing up and attending school, even the elementary schools had what we referred to as 'sports day.' This was a day to showcase your fitness and there was a winner for first, second and third place. We were motivated to capture the title and the ribbon.

I remember walking my children to school on their sports day and could over-hear what the older group of kids in front of us were saying. They asked each other if they were looking forward to the sports day and most replied with, "Naw, we all get the same ribbon at the end of the day, so what's the point?"

With that, it is important to teach our children how to motivate themselves to do their best, in all things, everyday. The real world does not see us as all equal and children need to develop self-esteem and confidence to go after what they want.

We also need to teach our children how to handle losing or rejection. We need to empower them as they learn to deal with their feelings of not being first. Identify with your child what their strengths are, maybe they are not the fastest runner on sports day and they didn't get the ribbon because their true talent is art, and they would surely win first prize for a painting, when the runner would not. Every child has something they are good at, and that is what parents need to focus on and build up.

Sometimes, children can lose their special talent because they are too busy trying to keep up to their friend's talents (or parents expectations) and when they cannot be as good, they feel defeated. Be sure to expose them to their unique talent and if they haven't discovered it yet, help them to find it. Teach them sportsmanship, teach them about losing gracefully and with dignity. These are life skills that will help them when they are older. Be a role model, show them how to pick themselves up, how to keep going and keep trying and not to take it personally, just use it as a growing through life tool.

> *"Parents need to fill a child's bucket of self-esteem so high that the rest of the world can't poke enough holes to drain it dry."* —Alvin Price

Teaching and developing your child's emotional health are parental responsibilities. Also, as a parent, teaching character building skills can make raising a child easier on you, the parent, and it enables open conversations with your children and builds their self-esteem. Children learn most of their life skills by the time they are five years old. That is before kindergarten, so for those first few years, do not be afraid of *not* making your child happy and *not* giving them everything they want.

During these years with my own children I was very firm and did not allow my children to sway me and my decisions. I realized fully that this was not a popularity contest for 'most liked parent' … your child's future depends on this! In being so firm with my children when they were young, yes… my children called me 'mean.' If your children do, please don't take this personally or as a label … they will forget in short order and it will not define the relationship you have with them. Sometimes a requirement of parenthood is to have a backbone. If you understand yourself first, have a clear vision of your parental responsibility, then be confident and own your position! Later when my kids were teenagers I asked them how 'mean' they thought I was and they don't ever remember saying that or thinking that. Another reason to do it when they are young.

In the next chapters I am going to go through a number of things that should be – actually *must* be – taught by the parents as this is not a responsibility that teachers or schools are required to teach.

Let's begin …

COMMUNICATION: TALKING, LISTENING AND THE HIDDEN MESSAGES

"What we sometimes see as a failure to behave properly,
Is actually a failure to communicate properly."
—Amanda Morgan

—————— Talking Communication ——————

"Be Impeccable with your words."
—Miguel Angel Ruiz

When we look at teaching our children to communicate, the best time to start is immediately. It is not so that the parent can communicate, it is for the child to communicate to the world.

The future is only a short distance away, and now is the time to be teaching life skills that will help them as a child and in their future years. A few years ago, when I was a facilitator for a parenting group, the greatest statement I heard from many of the parents is that their teen doesn't and won't talk to them, they cannot get anything out of their teen about what is happening in their life.

People are communicators, and yet we fail to communicate well. In today's world, it is more likely you will communicate more often by text and Instagram or Facebook. My goal is not to teach communication by these methods, my goal is to help you talk and listen to your child for a very real and bonding relationship.

The reason we start young is because we are putting our children in training. If we start communication young it just forms a part of who they are without even thinking of it, it is just a normal thing to talk to your parents, so we are developing the 'norm.'

We communicate by words, facial expression, body language and voice pitch. We also communicate by listening, active listening, hearing and understanding. Another way of communication is a little more mysterious and that is, hidden messages that are received by the child, from the parent.

> *"Speak clearly, if you speak at all; carve every word before you let it fall."* —Oliver Wendell Holmes

To begin, let's take a look at our words. It is so important that we are impeccable with our words as parents. So often our words come out of our mouth without any thought, and most of us can relate to a time we blurted something out only to wish it came with a delete button. The only way to fix this is to think before we speak, and for most of us, it is a good idea, but not our reality. Most adults can handle it if we just toss around our words but, for a child, it is very different. We need to be cognizant of our words.

When children are just little, quite often I hear parents tell the child to use their words when asking for something. This is a great lead into communication and you can start building manners such as, 'please,' and 'thank you.'

—— Keep the Door Open for Sharing ——

"The way we talk to our children becomes their inner voice."
—Peggy Omara

The child grows and gains new vocabulary and we need to use our vocabulary also. Remember, we can only teach what we can do. The parent needs to be able to communicate to the child in an age appropriate way, and that is for you the parent to determine.

Some of the problem is when we look at a three-year-old, the parents think and believe the child is too young to understand so they don't bother talking and teaching. Suddenly, the child is ten and when you ask how their day was, they just reply with 'fine' and the parent is wondering why the child is not talking to them more. The parent has missed several years of developing and teaching the 'talking' communication skill, and then has an expectation the child will resume when the parent has decided it's now a good time to talk.

The window has been closed by the child, the seams have been painted over and when the parent tries to jar the window open, it won't budge. This is not the fault of the child, they don't know better. The child was willing to learn and talk at three years old, at five years old, at seven years old but after that, perhaps the child felt a chill and closed that window.

With that said, if we want our children to talk to us, and we want to know what is happening in their life, ask yourself if you have created an environment that is safe for the child to speak up? Human nature is that we will choose to talk to someone that understands us, is non-judgemental and safe. Wouldn't you also choose to talk to someone like this? If we present ourselves to our children as never doing anything wrong, children will feel less comfortable telling you they made a mistake because, in their eyes you have never made a mistake and therefore you wouldn't possibly understand them. As such, they will likely seek out their friends to talk to, and the parent is left out.

Where it is appropriate, I suggest that we open ourselves up to our children and let them into our world even just a little bit. Tell them stories of the mistakes you made at their age and laugh about them with your children. This did two things for my relationship with my kids, first, they realized that I wasn't born as a parent, I was actually, once upon a time, a child just like them. This may seem odd but, your child didn't know you as a child so to them, you were born a parent. Second, because I let them into my life, sharing my memories, what I did at work, some gentle ups and downs I faced and how I handled them, the next thing I knew, they began to ask how my day at work was when I picked them up from school, and they really cared about my answer. It was a very cool feeling to have them care about my life too. It also made me a human just like them, to know that I am also capable of making mistakes and living to talk about them. The door is completely open now for sharing, both ways.

At dinner time with my children, they were not forced to eat if they were not hungry however, their dinner was put on hold in the fridge until they were hungry; I never made separate meals. I did request that they be present at the table, eating or not. I would ask them to tell me what the very best thing that happened to them today was. When they told me, I could then ask more probing questions and before you know it they were letting me in and telling me everything about their day. We would then go around the table and tell what the worst thing that happened that day. This would also let me know what troubles they were having and again, ask more questions.

Be Patient While They Learn

"Words have meaning. And their meaning doesn't change."
—Antonin Scalia

For younger children, they are a lot smarter than we think or give them credit for. Their minds are like sponges that soak up everything we give them, so let's fill them up! Yes, it is likely that you will have to repeat your lessons again and again, but laying the foundation early will make the teen years so much easier on the parent. Whatever we start the little ones with is what they will take with them into their teens and adulthood, so this is very important. Communication is essential for every aspect of life: friends, family, school, jobs and careers. Without it we all just flounder around and make the wrong assumptions.

"First learn the meaning of what you say, and then speak." —Epictetus

One of the best ways to communicate to your child is with your words and their meanings. Let's not forget the child is new to this world and all that is in it. Their mind is an empty board waiting to be painted with information. We are training them for the future. If you were training a pet, you would repeat and repeat the lesson until it was learned and then rewarded. Why do we give up so quickly in repeating these lessons with our children? We think they will grasp and understand immediately the first time and we need to be patient while they learn. All children will learn in their own time, just as they learned to walk in their own time.

The first rule and biggest is, if you say something to your child… mean it. That is worth repeating … if you say something to your child… mean it. If you say to your child to put the toys away, make sure they understand they need to put their toys away. If you the parent says 'no,' please mean it and stick to it. Once you don't stick to your words, you have lost the child. It doesn't mean you can't get the lesson taught to them, it just means it will be a harder lesson to teach later.

—— Explain What the Right Behaviour —— Looks Like

"Your child's behaviour is not about you.
It is because of you.
Whatever you put into them is what you will get out."
—Katrina Doxie

If we want our children to do as we say, perhaps we should look at the words we give them. For an example, let's use the word 'respect.' You tell a child to respect the rules and that is great but, how does the child know what the word 'respect' means and what are the behaviours that go with 'respect?' What are the consequences if the child does not 'respect?' If the meanings are not taught, the child will do what they think the word means, and when it is incorrect, the child is punished or the parent is mad at the child, and the child is left confused. As the child is new to the world and learning, they may not even know to ask questions about the word and the meanings and besides, it is not their responsibility, it is the parents' to teach.

If we want certain behaviours from our children it is important to tell them the word, explain the meaning and explain how that behaviour looks. If you have a small child and the word 'behave,' in order to teach the meaning of this we can start by saying, "it is important for you to behave tonight at your grandparents. Do you know what 'behave' means? It means that I need you to do as you are told to do, when you are told to do it." Then ask, "Does that make sense, do you understand what I am asking?"

From there the child will tell you what they know, and what they don't. Explain it in different ways until the child understands, and ask them to give you an example or, ask them to tell you what they think the word 'behave' means. Once you have achieved that, then you can tell them the consequences if they do not 'behave.' Ask them to describe what will happen if they don't 'behave.' This way, your child is more likely to understand what is expected of them, and you know they heard your words, instead of the child wondering whatever happened to the worm in the garden they found earlier in the day.

Stop, Don't and No

There are three basic words that carry so much power, and I felt it important that my kids know them and reacted to them. The words I taught them were Stop, Don't and No. There is a reason for these words and there is a reason your child needs to learn them and the urgency of them. It means, do not do this, and it means it now, not two hours from now or later, it means *now*. I told my children that even if they were tickling each other and having fun and one of them said any of these words, we must stop immediately. Even if you were both laughing and having fun, you don't know if suddenly you are hurting them or if they cannot catch their breath, so to avoid any serious consequences, stop immediately. It is also about personal boundaries and they must respect the word.

Let's discuss the word 'no.' Small word, big meaning. When parents say the word 'no' repeatedly, it becomes familiar and to some extent, ignored. We parents must not over-use this word as when we say it, we need it to carry some force. It is hard at times to say 'no' as, deep down we really do want to please our child and see them happy however, it is for everyone's sake to teach it, and stick with it. If you retract the word 'no' after it is said, by giving in and turning the no into a 'yes,' the 'no' becomes null and void. The next time you say it the child will believe it less and less. If you can stick to the 'no,' your life with the child will be a much better place.

> **"Saying 'No' does not always show a lack of generosity and that saying 'Yes' is not always a virtue."** —Paulo Coelho

Something I used to say to my children, and it worked well is, "No, I am sorry you are disappointed but, my answer to your request is no." I would then follow up with 'why' the answer is no. Telling them why you have made the decision to say no helps them understand, and helps them to resist approaching you one hundred times with… 'but, pleeeease???'

I would then tell them, "…for those reasons I am saying no, and this means that in three minutes from now, my answer will still be no. This means that two hours from now, my answer will still be no. Tomorrow, in three days, next week and next month, my answer will still be no. You may continue to ask me but you really don't need to bother, as my answer is still no and will always be… ?" … And let your child vocally add the word 'no' to finish the point.

By doing this, I gave my child no reason to keep approaching me with their plea for a yes. It is done and over. They did not wear me down to get a yes, and after that my children didn't bother to ask a second time. They knew where they stood, and they knew I meant what I said. This made it easy to get on with other things in life and move on without whining and a scene. They developed respect for the word 'no.'

We need to teach our children not just tell them. Teaching is interactive and not one sided. What is learned by the child if the parent just said, 'No, because I said so?' I only know this means the parent is boss, but I don't know why the parent said no. Do you think the child would learn more if instead the parent said, "No, because if you do, there is an immediate danger to yourself and others. Here is what can happen … do you still want to make that decision knowing what you know now?"

There is another reason why these three words are very important to be taught. Truly the first reason was to make my life easier as a single parent. It saved me valuable time not getting into a push/pull cycle that never seems to end until one gives in. Second, I realized these lessons were for now, the present, and also for the future in my children's life. Think about that. My son is with a girl and does something she is not comfortable with. All the girl has to say is, stop, don't or no. My son will immediately cease doing what is making her uncomfortable. It also gives my daughter a future voice to say to a boy, stop, don't or no. Her expectation is that he will because, that is what she was taught. If he doesn't respect her words, she knows this is not where she should be.

Teaching your child has future impact. As a parent, I would like to invite you to remember that.

> *"Kind words can be short and easy to speak, but their echoes are truly endless."*
> —Mother Teresa

There were other words that were not invited into my home and I taught them to my children. It wasn't that they couldn't use them ever, they just couldn't use them in my home. In fact, anyone coming into my home had the same rule, adult or child. There are some words that are just 'ugly' words and anyone coming to visit, knew that these words were not welcome in my home, they could leave them at the front door and pick them up again on their way out. Some of these words were 'stupid, shut up' and any expression that was racial or derogatory to another person. We issued new words that were acceptable like, instead of stupid, we used the word silly, and instead of shut up we used the term, be quiet. You have the right and permission to have your own group of words that you do not want to have expressed in your home. Also, remember to explain to your child why the use of these words is inappropriate and not acceptable.

—————— Embarrassing Moment ——————

"You have the right to remain silent,
Anything you say can, and will be,
Used against you by your child in a busy public setting."
—Unknown

Another example of communicating to a young toddler was with my daughter when she was only about three years old. It was a method of taking the time to let your child know where you are going, what is going to happen, and what you expect of their behaviour.

I had taken my daughter to a bank on a Friday late afternoon when of course, there was a long line waiting to get their transactions done for the weekend. This particular bank, had a little playhouse for the children to play in while the parents completed their business. Of course, I said to my little girl it was okay for her to play in the playhouse, and off she went.

I completed my banking and went to the playhouse to collect my daughter and asked her to come out, it was time to go. To my dismay, I hear a little voice saying, 'No!' I asked again that she come out and received the same word from my daughter. I was not impressed, and I was embarrassed as everyone in the bank line was watching and waiting to see how I would deal with this situation. After asking numerous times quietly, to minimize the attention I was receiving from the bank line, it became apparent that I would have to enter the little playhouse and bring her out myself.

I entered this little playhouse, let her show me what she was playing with and then told her we need to go, now. She once again very sternly said 'No!' I ended up grabbing her and carried her out kicking and screaming, I glanced at the bank line of customers and proceeded out the door and into the car. I was not a happy mother!

She was so angry with me for removing her that she carried on with the fight as I tried to buckle her into her car seat. Eventually, we were on our way, me frustrated and embarrassed, and her crying and screaming. I didn't know what to do and decided that I would never take my little girl to the bank ever again, and how dare the bank have a little playhouse for the kids! I did actually try to blame the bank for my daughter's behaviour! I would get a sitter and go alone from now on!

A Teachable Moment

"Tell me and I forget,
Teach me and I remember,
Involve me and I learn."
—Benjamin Franklin

During the time of us both having our tantrum, differently but still each of us was having a moment, I did realize that me yelling at her at this time, would be of no use as she would not hear me, and I also realized that blaming the bank for the playhouse was ridiculous. We both needed some time to cool off. Once we both became calm, I sat her down and asked if she remembered not coming out of the playhouse when I asked her to at the bank. She did. I knew then that she would at least follow what lesson I wanted to teach. I told her that her behaviour was not okay. Note, I did not tell her that 'she' was bad, I told her that her 'behaviour' was bad, explained why, and what I would expect her behaviour to be like next time.

Sure enough, weeks later I needed to go to the bank again. I really did consider getting a sitter for only a moment, and then realized that I needed to do something, as I cannot realistically simply avoid going to the bank with a child. So, I made a plan…

Before we left the house, I told her we were going to the bank, the one with the little playhouse. With the word 'playhouse' I knew I had her attention. I said, "Mommy has some banking to do and while I am busy doing that, you can go and play in the playhouse." I also told her, "When Mommy is finished her chore at the bank, I will come to the playhouse and tell you it is time to leave and you will come out of the playhouse the first time I ask."

I then broke it down for her. I said, "Where are we going?" She said, "To the playhouse."

"Correct," I replied. I asked, "Will you play in the playhouse?" and she lit up and said, "Yes!" I said that would be great fun! Then I asked, "When Mommy comes to the playhouse and says it is time to leave, what will you do?"

She replied, "Leave."

She had the answers and knew the behaviour because I took a moment to explain it to her – we were both on the same page. However, because of her age, I also knew that her retention of this conversation could easily get lost on the way to the bank, and also once she was inside the playhouse.

Repeat, Repeat, Repeat

"Sometimes in life,
Your situation will keep repeating itself
Until you learn your lesson."
—Brigitte Nicole

I then got her in the car, tucked into her car seat and started off for the bank. On the way to the bank, I asked again, "Where are we going?" and she said, "The playhouse." Again, I asked all the same questions as I did just before we left the house. She still had the right answers. Then, I repeated myself all the way to the bank, about a fifteen-minute drive. "We are going to the bank and you may play in the playhouse while Mommy does her business. When I come to the playhouse and say it is time to leave, you will come out of the playhouse." In order not to drive you crazy reading this book, imagine how many times I can say that in fifteen minutes! Over, and over, and over again.

When we arrived at the bank I asked the same questions again, before getting out of the car, "Where are we? What will you do when Mommy says it is time to leave?" She had the right answers again so, we proceeded into the bank and I took a deep breath.

Well, that day I got my banking done, went to the playhouse, said it was time to leave, and to my amazement, she walked out without an issue. We do better when we know better, by taking the time to communicate and explain where we were going, what is expected of their behaviour, we can avoid unwanted circumstances. I must also add, this was not the only situation that I used this technique, there were several when she was just a little toddler and each time, this worked.

Now time marches on and they get a little older, you can still ask them to do something as you did at the younger age. It is still important to let them know what you are expecting from their behaviour. At this age, there may be some pushback from the child. You can explain that you are requesting this behaviour for certain reasons, and explain what those reasons are. You can also say to the child that, you understand they may not want to do as you ask or agree with you, and that is okay, they don't have to agree but you have the expectation that they will follow through. If they don't, explain the consequences of not following through and ask them if they understand.

Get Into Their World

"Your child's world is just as valid and important as your own.
Understand it.
Respect it."
—Unknown

Another important part of communication with an older child is talking to them about their world. If we can show them that we are interested in their world, we can open locked doors. For a moment, put yourself in your child's shoes. Wouldn't you like it if there was a bridge between your parents' world and yours?

When my kids were about eight and ten, one of the popular singers or rappers at the time came out with a popular new CD. His rapping music was the rage and the kids were all listening to it. I knew this musician's work and I also knew it was full of lyrics that were not lyrics I particularly wanted my kids to absorb. I could have forbidden my children to listen to it but, that would be pointless because they could always listen at a friend's or school, wherever the music was playing. I could not actually stop them from listening to it, only in my own home perhaps. I decided to take a different approach and I went out and bought the unedited version of the CD. I chose to listen to it along with my children.

As we listened for a while, I separated the music from the lyrics. I told my kids that I actually understand why they like this, as I also liked the music part and the beat. Then, because I liked the music, which was part of their generation, I moved in their minds from old to current and we could start a conversation about the lyrics, how dark they seemed, perhaps what the artist was feeling at the time he wrote them. This led into a big conversation between us, and that was my motive. I wanted to talk to my kids first about what they were hearing and learning, so they would have my influence in their thoughts and perhaps a little more understanding of what they were listening to.

Take the time to approach subjects with your older children, let them know you are interested in their world, not just by asking about it, but by being in it. This will open the doors for more conversations during the teen years, a vital time to have open communication.

Mind The Volume

"Raise your words,
Not your voice.
It is rain that grows flowers,
Not the thunder."
—Rumi

We may from time to time raise our voice to our children. Usually by that time we feel the need for a release, and let it fly. I raised my voice only once with my daughter. To this day, she will tell you what grade she was in, and what day of the week it was. As it was the first time I had raised my voice to her, it scared her and her eyes went huge as my voice was raised. She was going to be late for school again, and I had had enough of waiting for her every day. That day when I dropped her off at school I felt terrible. Terrible that she was starting her day on a negative note and knowing this energy would stay with her all day. I apologized before she left the car, as I was sincerely sorry for my actions. The situation could have been handled differently and much better than yelling, however at the time, it just happened like it happens to so many parents.

The next day she was up early, her bed was made and we were early to school. I believe this reaction from her happened because, she hadn't heard me raise my voice and it meant something when I did. If you were to yell at your child daily for everything, it no longer carries the weight you are hoping for. The kids will shut out the noise because that is all it is for them now. It's like going out for dinner. If you do it five times a week, it's no longer special and becomes the norm. If you go out for dinner only once every now and then, it is something to remember. Be conscious of what you are saying and how you are saying it.

When a miscommunication occurs, is it the fault of the speaker or the listener? Sender or receiver? If we explain our words and associated behaviours and give the receiver an opportunity to ask questions for better clarification, then you are teaching your child the art of communication and understanding.

> *"Your children need your presence more than your presents."* —Jesse Jackson

Through communicating with my children, it also meant that I did not need to use bribes such as, 'If you do this, I will get you that.' If we communicate effectively, there are no lessons we teach, that would require a bribe.

Teaching good communication is a life lesson. It will help them in all aspects throughout their life. It is worth your time to cultivate good spoken communication.

> *"Texting is a brilliant way to miscommunicate how you feel, and misinterpret what other people mean."* —Unknown

Challenges in verbal communication come from exempting face to face, exchanging of words, and replacing them with a keyboard for texting. I do want to make clear, the face to face communication is still important and to make this time happen. I am not asking that text not be part of the communication, only that the face to face doesn't get forgotten. The world still operates face to face and just imagine for a moment what the world would be if we only used our keyboard. No more expression of voice, the sound of excitement or the sound of someone that is down and needs a lift up. If we only had emoji's to convey our feelings… what a sad world indeed it would be without expression.

Listening

> *"So when you are listening to somebody, Completely, Attentively,*
> *then you are listening not only to the words,*
> *But also to the feeling of what is being conveyed,*
> *To the whole of it, not part of it."*
> —Jiddu Krishnamurti

When my children were babies, I remember looking at them, holding them up and really looking at them and wondering, who are you in there? What will be your likes and dislikes? What toys will you prefer to play with? What will you want to be when you grow up? What will be your contribution to society? I really wanted to know who they were in that little body.

We as parents will never really know our child unless we listen to them, even from infancy. In fact, infancy is the easy part because they are so new and we just want to capture every little noise they make. Once they start to grow a little, and start discovering their thoughts, their voice and their words, we the parent tend to tune them out a little and complain they make too much noise. That noise is exactly what we should be tuning into and listening to because, they are communicating who they are.

To listen is to pay attention: be attentive, concentrate on what is being said. To understand is to grasp, absorb, and comprehend. In order to be a good communicator, we must also be good at listening and understanding.

When we listen to our children, no matter what the conversation is, starting from a small child, will either give the child validation and a sense of belonging and acceptance or, quite the opposite if we don't listen.

——————— Discover Who They Are ———————

"The first duty of love
Is to Listen."
—Paul Tillich

When we open the door to listen, to really listen to our children, we will discover who they are. This cannot happen without listening. If we do not listen, we will be left out of our child's life. If we will not listen, why should they talk to us? If they don't talk, we have no relationship with them and when they get to be a teenager, we have lost them completely. A simple choice to listen to what they have to say, without judgement of their thoughts and feelings, without trying to have them think differently, will determine the depth of your relationship with your child. Keep the conversation going by asking them questions about their thoughts, for example, "Then, what happened?" or "How did that make you feel?" or "What do you think would have been better if ...?" You can only ask these questions if you were listening in the first place. Try to not jump in and solve their problem or tell them they should do this or that, and don't make judgements. Trust that if they want your opinion, they will ask for it. Life is about learning and sometimes things need to be learned in different ways, than how you learned them.

Listening to your children at an early stage, and all through their growing years is one of the most important things we can do. Listening without actually hearing what they are saying, is meaningless to both parties. For example, imagine approaching your boss with an idea, an idea that you researched and truly believed was a great idea. Once you presented the idea, you looked into your boss' blank face, and you just knew what you said didn't get heard, because you were dismissed without any questions or comments. How would you feel?

Now think about a child telling you something that is important to them and you slough it off without acknowledgement. You think you are fooling your child but, in reality you are not.

When you listen to your children, you are brought into their world, the more you are attentive, the more they talk to you, it's human nature. How many parents do you hear say, "My kid never talks to me." Why would they if you don't actually listen to them? Recall a time when you entered an office to discuss your personal life, maybe it was a banker, a lawyer or the person that prepares your taxes. Upon entering the office, your professional person buzzes through to the receptionist, and asks that all calls be put on hold and to take a message. If you are like most, this makes you feel important. We do this in our professional life out of respect. Why don't we do this for our children?

Take a moment, forget about your phone and the housework. Give them their moment with you to express themselves, and open your worlds.

Listening Takes Time

"You cannot truly listen to anyone
And do anything else
At the same time."
—M. Scott Peck

I made a contract with myself when my kids were young and it was, if my kid's lips were moving, I was listening. Many of our talks would last for hours and hours. Yes, I took that much time to listen. It brought us close, I became a trusted sounding board for them. They had permission to talk about everything and anything they wanted. This carried on through the teen years, and when my daughter was considering breaking it off with her boyfriend, we sat on the couch for five and a half hours talking about it, and I asked questions that would help her to figure out her own answer and conclusion. I would let her talk, without interrupting (so important!), let the child's thoughts flow. When her thought was finished, then I would ask questions to help her explore her feelings and beliefs; 'How did that make you feel? What if you were married and that happened, would that be okay? How would it affect you? If that happened to your best friend, what would be your advice to them?'

> *"Children who are allowed time to think for themselves, learn to have faith in their own problem solving abilities."* —Unknown

By asking questions and listening to the answers, the parent rarely needs to be involved with solving the problem for them. The child will learn to answer their own questions and because they did it on their own, it will be empowering for them, and they will grow so much more because they were not just told how to handle a situation, it puts them in control. They can learn to solve their own issues with the help of a trusted sounding board. I must point out, if you are talking about a situation that may be harmful to your child or to another child, more direct input may be required from the parent. A situation like that, is one you may never know about if you do not open up the communication door early in their life.

Something to consider while we are on the subject of listening is, when we listen we also validate the other. How would it feel to you to have someone else know what was happening in your child's life because they saw it on Facebook or Twitter? The internet may know more about your child's life than you because, that's where children can turn for validation and actually feel like they have been heard.

> *"I love when conversations and energies just flow. Not Forced. Not Coerced. Just Present."*
> —Dau Voire

Many times the talks I had with my children started at night and we would talk into the wee hours of the morning. Several times it was a school night and the conversations were very important. Yes, there were times we were tired in the morning but, we still made it to school and on with our day. We can get over being tired, but the opportunity for that particular conversation may not have come again, and I never wanted to lose a moment I couldn't get back.

When the kids were in their teens, I told them I would always pick them up and bring them home, no matter how late or how far away they were. This way, I was able to meet all their friends, see how the friends treated each other and how they treated my kids. I would offer to drive any of the kids home, and when they all piled into my vehicle, it seemed as though they forgot I was there and driving them. They would all talk freely about the goings on of the evening. I was getting plugged in... I didn't interrupt their flow of conversation, I only listened. Best of all... I knew they were all safe at home at the end of the evening and that, is worth a few moments of my time and a few dollars in fuel for the car.

Had I told them to find a ride home or take the bus or taxi, the next day when I would ask how their evening was, I would simply get, 'It was good,' and the conversation would be over.

Cultivate the safety of your child to express themselves to you about anything and everything. Tell them about you too, so they know you were vulnerable and learning at their age, just as they are. Sometimes there may be things you don't want to hear but, it is better to hear them than not be a part of their lives.

How good are your listening skills?

—————— Love Languages and the —————— Benefit of Knowing Them

"Just because someone doesn't love you the way you want them to, Doesn't mean they don't love you with all that they have."
—Unknown

My son recently told me that a profound time for him was when I sat them both down to discover what they needed most from me, and if I was being successful in meeting all their needs. Just as you have needs that need to be met in your relationships, our children do to... why wouldn't they?

I had recently read a book titled, "The Five Love Languages" – written by Gary Chapman. I thought at first it was a book directed at marriages however, after reading it, realized it is good for all relationships. I wanted to ask my children what their love language was and I didn't want to just assume I was hitting their needs. When I asked them to put in order the most important language to the least important language from the list of five, I was surprised at what their answer was.

The Five Love Languages consist of: Words of Affirmation, Quality Time, Receiving Gifts, Acts of Service, Physical Touch.

Make sure when you do this exercise with your children, you understand both sides. Listen and communicate. Discover what the other person needs in order to feel loved, and do that.

It is interesting that we can look at this and say well… this is how I show it. It's not about how you choose to show it, it is about the other persons needs. If you show love by doing Acts of Service but the other person needs Quality Time, you will miss the point.

This exercise was not only enlightening, it also opened up a great discussion between us and brought us so much closer together. I encourage you to discover your child, and what their personal needs are, and to listen carefully!

———————— Hidden Messages ————————

"Judge not by the form of the messenger,
But the form of the message."
—Richard Bach

Another area of communication is the messages that we send, and are received by our children when we are not paying attention. By not communicating and not listening, they are hidden messages.

Parents should be very aware of what they leave in their wake by not acknowledging their children. Remember that children are capable of picking up on numerous messages.

Most parents these days work, whether you are a traditional family with mother and father, or a single parent. For argument's sake let's say you work from nine to five. What is left of the time you have with your child? The morning time before work is filled with getting ready yourself, getting the child ready and packed for school or daycare, packing lunches, getting breakfast on the table, etc. Then after your work time is finished, you are picking up the child, getting home, unpacking, preparing the evening meal, cleaning up, more lunches to pack, notices from school to go over, bath time and story reading for bedtime, and not included is running to sports practices and dance lessons.

During these busy times, your child will approach you with a question or just to acknowledge what they are doing. Your mind is full of the next task and you may glance at your child and nod however, you are not really present. You just have to get on to the next task, so you can all go to bed.

Picture yourself as the child, watching as everything is getting done around you but no one has time to pay attention to you. No one is listening to your needs or cares. If you were that child, how would you be feeling?

I remember the tugs at my pants because there was something my children wanted me to hear or see. I also remember giving them a flitting glance, and doing the 'uh-huh' ... with no clue later what they were trying to communicate to me. Then one day I woke up. I questioned myself as to what might my child be feeling when I do this? What is the message that I am giving to them? I didn't like my answer.

> *"People may hear your words, but they feel your attitude."* —John C. Maxwell

We the parents, think we are doing okay when we loosely acknowledge our child in a busy moment but, what is the message we are sending to them and how are they perceiving this message? On the outside, the child may appear to be fine however, internally the message they have received is, 'I am not important' or, 'I am not worthy' or, 'I am not enough.' Perhaps we are communicating that they are less important than the laundry, dishes, cooking, lunches or whatever has our attention at the moment. The child internalizes they are less important than the task. Understand this is how we end up shaping our children's perceptions, perceptions that can last a lifetime and if they do, let's hope they are the good ones. Perceptions made from feelings rather than reality can be some of the hardest to make better.

Some children will withdraw and start believing and accepting they are not important, other children will act out with tantrums to get the attention they are craving. Yes, children crave attention, it is part of their growth process. When they realize at a young age, they have to actually compete with a task for importance, their perception is one of competition. Sometimes this can lead into bully behaviour or another negative trait. Parents are mortified to discover their child is a bully when no one else in the family is even remotely like that; they don't bully their child. Where it comes from is the perception that they are not enough, or important enough. They are fighting for their position, and recognition, and the majority of children have no idea why they are fighting so hard.

Let me ask a question. Why do we work so diligently, we rewrite reports so they are exact and will please our boss, or we go the extra mile, volunteer overtime and sometimes cancel personal plans to make sure our job is done to perfection, and meets the deadline. Mainly, we do it because we want the recognition from our boss for a job well done. So really... we are not unlike our children in this forum, are we? You want recognition from your boss and/or client, just as a child wants it from their mother or father.

Let's look at what messages we can pass without realizing. For example, you have just arrived home from work, and you are tired and just need to unwind from your day before getting into the next part of your day, called family time. Your child jumps up on you and wants your attention but, you excuse them because you just need some time to yourself to unwind, and request a half hour to relax before engagement. Suddenly the phone rings … it's your boss or co-worker and they are asking you to do something right away. Somehow you find the energy instantly to do the task requested of you. Your child is now watching you come to life with a phone call, and recognizes that you did not come to life for them. You have just given your child a hidden message, and an important one.

> *"The hardest thing of all is when pain is hidden behind a mask of calm."* —Sergei Lukyanenko

Why do we put business and clients ahead of our own family, and why is it so much more important than raising your child? Children are most eager to learn, especially from their parents. With this action, you have just taught your child something important but, you won't even know you just taught them this. In a child's mind, this child is now 'less than' because when the 'boss' calls we jump, when the 'child' calls, we don't jump.

I understand we need to pay attention to our jobs, it is how we manage and pay our bills and send our children to school and all the activities they do. What if we just took a moment to look our child in the eye and explain, 'You are very important, however, I am just in the middle of something and need to finish. Please keep your thought and I will give you my full attention as soon as I can.' Then follow through and go back to your child and ask them to tell you what was on their mind. Do this when the time is better, and they can have your full and undivided attention. Because you have acknowledged the child and their need, you respected the child and in return, the child can respect what you need to get done, knowing they have not been overshadowed by an unknown.

It is important to follow up, if you do not, the trust will be broken and they will once again see themselves as non-important. At least this way, they still know you want to hear them, and it also teaches them that they cannot always have first position, and to be patient. Valuable lessons for sure. As we want to hear and validate our children, we also do not want to create a culture where the child believes they are first always, it can lead to the child believing the world revolves around them, and that will not serve them well in later years.

Yes, I agree, sometimes life is busy and complicated in our adult world but, also remember the child does not live in our adult world, and to them each moment is important, and each discovery of this world is important.

We don't have to agree with our kids all of the time but, we do have a responsibility to at least understand our children. We need to understand how they feel about their lives. With understanding, we are better equipped to help guide them through the tough times and good times, and when they de-rail, this will help them to get back on track.

> *"How it seemed like you could see everything,*
> *but certain things were blocked out, hidden."*
> —Sarah Dessen

The hidden messages received by children are exactly that, they are hidden because it is a feeling based on actions, not something tangible. It can take years for a parent to even find out they exist in the child. For example, a parent watches a child fold the laundry, and the parent decides they don't like the way it is turning out so, the parent takes it from the child and says, "Let me do this." The child may internalize this as they are not capable, and the 'not capable' snakes through their thoughts on other tasks in their mind. Years later, the laundry is given to the child to fold again and the immediate reaction from the child is, 'I can't do this.' The term, 'I can't do this' also perpetuates into other areas of the child's mind and thoughts, until it develops a self-belief.

Parents can be blind to the messages they send their children. That is why it is so important to be conscious of our actions. The child then tells the parent they cannot fold the laundry because they can't do it right. The moment the child is talking about is long ago in the past, and the parent doesn't remember anything about it yet, for the child it was a pivotal moment. This pivotal moment will be a direct influence on how the child views themselves and/or limits the child's beliefs about themselves, and carries forth into what the child chooses to do, or not to do, with their lives.

So many parents just say they don't understand their children or why they do the things they do. Perhaps it is because they didn't take the time to understand and listen to their children. Start early and never underestimate the power of the parent's actions, on influencing our children's mind.

THOUGHTS, FEELINGS AND INTUITION

"Sometimes our thoughts and feelings are our most prized possessions...
And then there are times to let go of your possessions
And wander"
—Saul Williams

Thoughts

"If you realized how powerful your thoughts are,
You'd never think a negative thought again."
—Peace Pilgrim

As adults, we have thoughts. We have many. How many are good, and how many are bad? How long do we keep the good thoughts with us in comparison to how long we keep the negative thoughts rolling around in our brain?

Watch the news on television and see how much of it is positive, and how much of it is negative, and why don't we have a news program that is all positive news? Because, people are basically attracted to drama. Drama causes stress and so why do we choose this day after day? Is it because it makes us feel better that someone out there is having a worse day than we are? What is the attraction?

If we don't manage our thoughts, they become too familiar with being in the negative state. It's like doing the same exercise over and over, our body makes adjustments for it but, no other part of our body gets a workout. You now have one large muscle, and the other 640+ muscles go limp. This is what can happen to our mind if we don't stop thinking the same negative thoughts over and over.

If we have a great day and everything goes right, we are in a feeling of euphoria for the day! Yay for us! If something goes sour one day… we can carry that baby in our thoughts for weeks, and even months. What are we doing and why are we doing this? Life is not meant to be a dark hole for our thoughts to bring us down with a kaboom!

Now as children, let's look at what they see. When they are small they have not developed the positive and negative thoughts, and usually are in just bliss that they are here. Ever watch a child laugh a real belly laugh over something and we cannot figure out why it's so funny? I remember walking down the driveway with my daughter who was about a year old. As I held her I stopped to pick a flower growing along the path, and when I did, she started laughing the belly laugh. It made me laugh so I did it again to see if it was a coincidence. Sure enough, another flower picked and another belly laugh. This was so entertaining I did it until I had a complete bouquet.

She was in the moment, not worried about what her hair looked like, if she was wearing the right outfit for the outing, if her shoes matched or that perhaps she forgot to brush her teeth.

Nothing was interrupting her mind about the future or the past, she was just in the moment and loving it. Because I was with her, I was also in the moment, and nothing in the world mattered than what was happening at that moment.

> *"The happiness of your life depends on the quality of your thoughts."* —Marcus Aurelius

As parents, we should be aware of our thoughts and the influence they have over our lives. No matter what happens in a day, no matter how many perceived bad things happen, there will always be something positive that happened, or a positive lesson learned... we should start looking for the positive and dwell there for a while, and let the negative stuff go. This is about training ourselves to get rid of the drama, and focus on the positive. Believe it or not, it takes the same amount of energy to feel good as it does to feel bad so, why would we choose to feel bad and not good... or even great?

Your thoughts will control your environment and your environment is where your child is living. Do you really want your child to be a negative nelly or, do you want them to have a positive outlook on life, one where they can be as powerful as they want, and accomplish anything they put their minds to. I know which one I would choose.

> *"Our mind is like a garden, our thoughts are the seeds, you can grow flowers or you can grow weeds."* —Ritu Ghatourey

I wanted my children to be aware of the world and some of the issues in it. I did not want my child to live with worry, jealousy, or fear that negative thoughts create. I wanted them to live in a world that is empowering, and if something goes wrong, oh well… let's just move on and let it go because, worry and stress cannot change it. I didn't want people or media trying to influence my children to believe in the power of negative. When they were little I told them they could do and be anything they wanted, and I didn't want that message to disappear because we carry dark clouds with us. Bring on the sunshine! A positive brain will succeed, a positive brain will be happy, a positive brain will attract positive… everything!

Develop a habit with your children to find the positive in each day and each lesson. Train their minds to go to good places and practice gratitude for it. Your thoughts become your feelings and as Goutama Buddha puts it, *"**What you think, you create. What you feel, you attract. What you imagine, you become.**"*

Feelings

"Feelings are much like waves,
We can't stop them from coming,
But we can choose which one to surf."
—Jonatan Martensson

Something that we all have and share is our feelings. It is important to know our own feelings as well as our children's, know what triggers them, and it is helpful if we can navigate them.

Feelings are best described as an emotion. They are a part of us however, they can also be controlled by us. There are a plethora of feelings any of us can feel and for the purpose of this book, I would like to keep it as simple as possible, and in relation to raising children.

When I say that we can control our feelings, I am reminded about a time when my children were very small, about four and two years old. There was a huge storm off in the distance, and I knew that it would be upon us fairly soon. Storms for many people can be scary, nerve-racking and not pleasant. My children had not seen a storm before and I knew whatever reaction I put out was the reaction they would absorb and assume. Knowing this, I also had thoughts that I did not want to deal with children who were frightened and scared, and spend the rest of the day trying to calm them down.

> *"If you will stop feeding your feelings, then they will stop controlling you."* —Joyce Meyer

I could hear the roll of the thunder off in the distance and a few flashes of light broke in the sky. It was time for me to look at myself first: was I frightened? Was I calm? I asked myself, how can I handle this so that my children are not scared. Whatever they felt this time with their first storm would likely stay with them a lifetime. I chose at that moment to not be afraid of the storm, I was calm. An important message here is that I made a choice to be calm. That is the beauty of feelings, we have the power to manage them with just a simple choice.

I huddled with the kids, we had blankets around us and we were together in a safe and comforting place. We looked out in the distance through the window at the approaching storm. I asked that they be quiet so we could hear the party going on in the sky!

The storm banged and thunder rolled and flashes of light broke up the grey sky! I remained excited and said, "Wow, listen to how much fun the sky is having! There is a big noisy party going on up there with fireworks too!" My children's eyes were big at the new sounds but they looked at me having fun with it, and followed my reaction. They laughed and giggled every time there was a boom! Before it came too close, we all went outside to see it more clearly and hear how loud it was getting. We watched and laughed for a few minutes before going inside again. To this day, my children actually like a good storm and say there is something cozy about it.

The purpose of this story is to show you that you can have your child feel differently about things purely by your demonstration of how you, the parent, handles it and feels it. Had I allowed myself to be scared, the chances are my children would also be scared of storms. Please feel free to input your own scenario, this story is not just intended for 'storms.' We have a capacity to look at our own behaviour and change it with nothing more than a choice, and so is the same for many of our feelings.

My children now adults, know how to identify with their feelings. They don't let the feelings control them or their life but, they do ask themselves questions to understand why they feel a certain way about something. Sometimes, the feelings are a nudge that we need to look at ourselves and ask, why are we bothered by a situation that has my feelings going crazy, is there something within myself that I need to look at and possibly change, and what is the growth lesson in all of it?

On the other side, let's dwell in the feelings of being loved, of feeling secure and safe and cherish the feeling of... a good, make your eyes water... kind of laughter that raises our vibration to a new height. Seeing your child feeling happy, strong and alive with sparkling eyes, and an energy about them that could power up a small city is, for a parent... beautifully mesmerizing.

—— We Cannot Tell Others How to Feel ——

"Emotional pain cannot kill you,
But running from it can.
Allow. Embrace.
Let yourself Feel
Let yourself Heal.
—Vironika Tugaleva

It is important not to tell your child how to feel about a certain situation. As an adult, do you want people telling you how to feel about something? Likely not. We all have our own feelings, and are quite entitled to them. As a parent, our responsibility is not to tell our children how to feel but, instead to help them manage their feelings. Help them to understand them, and how they have the power to make them change if they are feeling bad.

When I was growing up, I had some underlying feelings about not fitting in to my family. As I grew into adulthood, I recognized that I had never dealt with my feelings about being adopted. All I could remember were family and friends telling me not to be sad about being adopted because, I had a great family now. It is true that my heart should have been filled with gratitude, and actually it was very much. The part I struggled with was, and purely my own feelings on this, I was at one point a mistake or my mother would not have given me away. When I wanted to acknowledge this, I was shut down by everyone around me, and never truly was able to have my own feelings on this.

When I was in my thirties I developed a condition called fibromyalgia. I was in pain in every joint in my body, what normally would have taken me thirty seconds to do, now took minutes. At the time that I was going through this, I had just found my birth family and was trying to put all the pieces in my life together so they fit in some way. There were so many emotions I felt at the same time, my head and heart were both confused. I tried to suppress these feelings because I was being told to do just that.

I realized that I needed to deal with my own feelings about this. Keeping in mind that not all adoptees feel as I do, again these were my feelings. I knew I had to get mad about the situation so that I could release all the pressure of these feelings, and finally be free and forgive. I gave myself permission to tell myself that I was a mistake at the beginning of my life story. I want to note that *no one* is a mistake, I just needed to deal with my personal negative feelings. I had to face them to eliminate them, and so I told myself that I was a mistake and I was not wanted by my mother. I allowed myself to get mad and beat up pillows, cry as long and as hard as I needed to. It was a release, and a very good one. The angry feelings that I had been storing up for years melted away, and when I became calm and accepting of being adopted, the fibromyalgia disappeared also. I came to a calm and peace and acceptance about it, and in return I regained my health. I was finally at peace.

> *"Don't rescue your child from a challenge. Teach them how to face it."* —Dr. Laura

The reason I tell this story is because, when we tell someone how to feel about something, we are limiting them, we are causing more damage than we realize. It may not be recognizable at the moment, but it is something that will come out eventually.

If your child feels a certain way about something, I recommend you listen, try to understand their feelings from their point of view and talk to them about it. Allow your child to have their own feelings, they are their own person, and these things come up to teach us lessons and our lessons in life are all different. When they are young, we can teach them how to see their feelings, how to identify with a lesson and celebrate the lesson learned.

Our feelings are not there to blame someone else for. If someone does or says something hurtful to us, it is not an opportunity to point a finger at someone else, it is an opportunity to point the finger at ourselves and ask, 'Why is this bothering me? What do I need to look at within myself, otherwise this wouldn't be bothering me.'

Lessons can be hard but they are necessary. Without them we do not grow. This is a blessing. Basically, allow others including your children to have their own feelings, they are entitled to this. Before telling your children how to feel, perhaps we can learn more about them and ourselves if we just stop and listen to why they feel what they do. Our job as parents is not to tell them they are wrong, we are here to empower them and the best way to do that when feelings are in the middle, have them explain, accept what they are saying, and help to guide them through. When we shut down the feelings of others, we are disabling them, again, it could result in the child not feeling worthy and being confused about their feelings. Feelings are real, we just have to navigate them so they also don't control our lives. If we take some time to listen and care about another's feelings, we may be surprised, and we may just learn something about them and ourselves. A gift indeed.

Intuition

So, as we navigate feelings there is one more invaluable feeling we need to teach our children, starting at a young age. This feeling is one that needs to be heard loud and clear and understood. This feeling is called our Intuition. How miraculous that our bodies were developed with this amazing device, our own personal alarm bell. Along with that, our bodies also come equipped with a mind, and the mind can try to convince us that the mind is stronger however… the intuition will always be wiser…

As adults, we understand that feeling that goes on inside of us when something is not quite right, whether that is about another person or a circumstance, some call it a 'spidy sense.' We tune in to this later in life and quite often we look back and think to ourselves, 'I knew that but, I just didn't listen to the feeling that was warning me.' How many regrettable things could we have avoided if we paid attention to this little 'feeling' that something is not as it seems.

Children can learn concepts at a young age, and so for my child's own protection, I began to teach this when my children were very young. I identified the feeling within. That feeling in the middle of your tummy that makes you feel worry or not at peace. You can use examples that young children can relate to. Ask your child how they felt when they did something they knew was wrong, and they feared they would get in trouble. Ask your child to tell you how their body felt.

It is important to have your child identify with the feeling so that it becomes common, and they can pick that feeling apart from others. Ask them how their body would feel if they entered an unfamiliar room that was dark and they heard a strange noise. Would their body feel like going in further to find the noise or, would it tell them to run and get out? Would it tell them to run and get out but, they would feel so curious they would ignore that run feeling and go further. Choose your own scenario that your child can relate to, to conjure up those feelings.

This is where the learning begins. Teach and identify the feelings and tell them they need to be very cautious about ignoring that 'run' feeling. Our bodies and our minds were created in such a way that we have warning bells. Where they prove difficult is when we decide to ignore them, and let our minds override the natural alarm.

> *"Always trust your gut. It knows what your head hasn't figured out yet."* —Unknown

We have all seen on TV shows where we know a person should get out, and they don't and our heart races, that is part of the buy-in of the show. We have also seen the shows, the documentaries, where someone went somewhere they shouldn't have, and something unpleasant happened. Many of these people will say, 'I knew I shouldn't have' or, 'If only I listened to my intuition' things would be better and different.

We are all full of choices, we make more choices in a day than we realize. What we need to do is, awaken in our children the ability to make the best choice in certain circumstances. We will not always make the right ones, but at least we can have our interpersonal alarm bell go off, and know what it means.

Knowing and understanding our alarm bell is so important for children. In this day and time of abductions, kidnapping, drugs, and a number of other terrible things that can happen to innocent children, this bell, if taught to use it, can save their lives. As a parent, at one time or another, you will teach your children not to go with strangers, which at times can be difficult for the child if the stranger is offering something that the child wants, and this alarm bell intuition is your backup as a parent, by teaching intuition you have given your child a second chance.

Other ways this can be important for your child, is when they start to venture out on their own, usually in their early teens. My daughter wanted to go to an outdoor concert in the city where we lived. I knew she was ready to venture out on her own, she had been taking the bus on her own and always followed the rules of 'call me' when you get there. She had earned the responsibility to go to town with a friend, to hear a concert.

Before she left, we went over the intuition button. I told her that the minute her internal alarm went off, she should leave immediately, call me, and I will pick her up. I asked that she please not ignore it even if they were having fun, and to help me help her, to be safe. I also said that even though everything around you seems fine, if this alarm goes off, don't ignore it even if you look around and things are normal. I explained that things can change in a second from good to worse, and even if nothing happened after you leave because of your alarm bell, it doesn't mean that nothing happened, just that you avoided something, and you may not even ever know what it was.

So, she was at the concert with her friend, and about half way through, I got the call. She had left the concert because something didn't feel right, she was at a Starbucks and would wait there for me to get her. After I picked her up, I thanked her for paying attention to the alarm and she has proven to me she is gaining maturity, and that I can trust her.

Once they have done something to gain your trust, have listened and followed your direction, please make sure you take a moment and tell your child how proud you are. This is imperative to perpetuate this behaviour again.

I took my daughter and her friend home that night and the next day, we heard that a fight involving several teens took place and the police did show up. Naturally, I talked about this with the girls, and once again, said how important it is to get away when the alarm bells go off.

On another note, intuition can be used by parents and brought into conversation when explaining to your child, why you are making the decision to say no to a particular request from your child. Another example of this was when my daughter was sixteen, and only a few weeks into her sixteenth year.

She approached me to ask if she could go away with a bunch of friends, including her boyfriend, for a weekend to a big city. Even though my first reaction internally was, 'absolutely not!', I always asked they tell me why this is important for them, what will be their plan, and how will I get hold of them.

If we just blurt out a 'no' without hearing them, they assume we don't understand them or care about their lives, and even go so far as to accuse the parent of sabotaging their life and friends. Quite untrue but, realistic in the teens eyes, as this is how they see their life. We do care about their life, so at times, before saying no immediately, even though it will be your final answer, ask them to tell you more and that you will consider it. When you finally do deliver your 'no' to them, at least they know you have considered it, and they are more likely to hear your decision when you explain why they are not going.

In this case, because she was taught the importance of intuition, it also meant that I could now use this on my children if I felt the warning alarm. As she knows the feelings and how right they can be, I was able to tell her that even though she has given me a plan of the weekend which I appreciate, I was just not comfortable as my alarm bell was going off. I told her I trusted her and her friends but, I did not trust the situation and my intuition was agreeing with me. I told her it is my first job to keep her safe as a parent, and that even after considerable deliberation I must listen to my alarm bells, and I just could not give her permission to go.

I also told her that I understand how she was feeling, as I can recall a time in my life I wanted to do something similar at her age, and was also not able to go. I told her I get this seems like the most important weekend and that she would feel left out if the other kids went without her. By relating to her, it gave her no reason to say I didn't understand and took that argument away. I also told her that not being able to go this weekend, would not define the rest of her life. Now she is older, and I did ask how that felt not to go, and she doesn't even remember asking about it. It did not define her life so parents, please don't be afraid to say no and explain your intuitive reasons.

Teach your children young about their internal alarm bell as it will keep them safe and help them make good choices. Also, don't forget about your own parental alarm bell, and use it to help a child understand your reason for saying 'no.'

VICTIM AND EMPOWERMENT

"Stop validating your victim mentality.
Shake off your self-defeating drama and
Embrace your innate ability to recover and achieve."
—Dr. Steve Maraboli

Victim

"When you're in the stays of the victim,
You don't really touch reality.
You're touching your thoughts about reality."
—Michael Beckwith

The word victim has many negative qualities, and yet I have watched so many parents and children get stuck in this world of believing they are a victim, and it can have a serious impact on lives. Feeling like a victim is essentially the feeling that the world or events are happening against you, a feeling of being duped. It is when you take those events and believe they are personally happening to *you*. However, we do have the power to see things differently and not live as a victim.

The strength of our emotional health will play a big part in determining whether or not we live with a victim mentality. Many people will never be able to get themselves from being a victim, to being a person of power. One of the greatest realizations for us is that we do not live in our circumstances, unless we choose to. It is as simple as a choice.

> *"Self pity is easily the most destructive of non-pharmaceutical narcotics. It is addictive, gives momentary pleasure and separates the victim from reality."* —John W. Gardner

Being a victim or the 'poor-me-pity-party,' takes away so much of your life that you could have enjoyed. Friends may join you in your pity party however, usually they don't stay long. When you are stuck in the victim role, you are also usually blaming everyone else for your being stuck there. Problem is, everyone else has moved on, getting on with their life and the only person that is feeling bad, is the person stuck as the victim. Unless we make a choice to remove ourselves from the victim role, we simply do not grow emotionally, and stay stuck.

Make it Better!

"Every test in our life makes us bitter or better,
Every problem comes to break us or make us.
The choice is ours whether we become Victim or Victor."
—Robert Tew

Even in your role as a parent now, you can use the excuse that you cannot parent well because, you were not parented well, and stay in that frame of mind while your kids grow up. Or, you can make a choice and tell yourself that you didn't have the best upbringing but, that won't stop you from doing everything you can to give your children a better start.

We are the ones that control our minds and thoughts. We can tell ourselves to do good or, not to do good. If we choose the negative, we will receive the negative results with no one to blame but ourselves.

We need to teach our children that life doesn't always go as planned, and it is not so much what is happening, as it is how we handle it. We cannot change other people, we are responsible for how we treat ourselves, and it is our responsibility to teach people how to treat us. We can tell others what is not acceptable, and do it respectfully.

If someone chooses to be nasty to us, we do not have to be a victim and then treat others in a nasty way too. If someone treats us nasty, we can take that energy and choose to help someone else that has been treated badly and treat them well. That way, we are no longer the victim and have regained personal power by helping another.

-------- Raise a Hero not a Bully --------

"A Hero is any person
Really intent on making this
A better place for all people."
—Maya Angelou

This world is a world that does not need bullies. What inspires bullies is their need for everyone around them to feel as bad inside as they do about themselves. This manipulation to bring others in to suffer with the victim role can be an easy one to fall into. We need to teach our children not to be bullies, and how to avoid the manipulation to be sucked into someone else's victim role. A victim will seek company – teach your children not to be that company. Inspire your child to do good for others, take care of the ones less fortunate, and you will raise a hero.

When my son was in high school and amongst the 'popular' crowd, he came home from school to tell me that he missed his afternoon classes. Of course, I asked him why. He said that another boy was being bullied and stuffed in his locker. My son went to him to see if he was all right, and he could tell the boy was near tears but was being strong. My son said, "Let's go get some Skittles and we can talk."

They left school, got some Skittles and a Slurpee, and went back to the school to sit and talk. After they chatted for a while, it became clear to my son that the boy wanted to be more like him. My son told the boy, "Do not try to be like me. There are things you can do so much better than I can. I can do sports but you man, you're an artist!" My son told him all of his unique and wonderful attributes, and what makes him awesome, and that he is better to embrace all of his talents as those will take him where he needs to go in life.

As a mom, hearing this made me proud of my son and the person that he is… his character. The teacher did catch them in the hallway, not in class and asked what they were doing. Once my son explained, the teacher was also moved by my son's actions, and reminded my son that the next day was 'anti-bullying' day.

> *"When someone is cruel or acts like a bully, you don't stoop to their level. No, our motto is, when they go low, we go high."*
> —Michelle Obama

Teach your child they are not better than others or too good to help someone else. Without learning the ability to take responsibility for themselves, they can end up in a lifetime of blame, blaming everyone and everything else for where their life has taken them. The truth is, we are only responsible for our own choices, not the choices of others. If we get stuck in the cycle of blaming others for our choices and problems, we can also be best friends with feeling depressed and believing that life is not worth living because the world is just unfair to us.

This boy could have lived each day at school being the victim. Sometimes it is not until someone steps up and helps them decide they don't need to be there, that each of us has something special to offer the world. Build them up and they will grow to be tall and strong.

—————— Empowerment ——————

"When you know yourself, you are empowered.
When you accept yourself, you are invincible."
—Tina Lifford

YOU are a Rock Star! YOU are limitless! YOU are amazing!
YOU are a warrior! YOU can do anything!

Start telling yourself this and other wonderful things about yourself. You are all these incredible, powerful affirmations! How do I know this? I know because you have not made it this far in life without believing in any of this at one point or another. You have accomplished something in your lifetime that made you say an internal, 'Wow! That was me, I did it! I feel fantastic! I feel like I can do anything!'

There has also been a moment or two or three or more in your life where you were so proud of yourself that it made you feel like you could take on the world. You did or thought something that gave you courage to dig in, go deep and find the warrior within. You have strength beyond that of your conscious mind. When you have been faced with a difficult time, one that you thought you would never get through… guess what… you did get through, and here you are! You are stronger for the experience, you are wiser, you are more confident and you know that deep down, you really can get through anything life gives you.

If you need to, put up little reminder sticky notes on the mirror, on your fridge, in your fridge, on your closet door, on the dashboard of your vehicle and keep reminding yourself that you are incredible, exactly how you are. Get it into your DNA. You don't have to tell the world, they will see it and believe it by the way you live, and when your light shines on those around you, you will inspire them to reach up and be all that they were meant to be, it is called the 'ripple effect.'

> *"Your time as a caterpillar has expired. Your wings are ready."* —Donna Pisani

Those around you most of the time, are your children. Let them soak up your brightness, your awesomeness, your fearlessness. Your children are watching you and learning from you. What you put out they will catch, a family shares everything from colds and flu to attitudes and happiness. Let your positive inspirational attitude take over your child like a bouquet of flowers sucks up water. Feed your children with positive beliefs about themselves, without limits. Your world has infinite possibilities, and so do your children...

Wake up every morning and realize that today is the present, and the future. We may know where we will be at certain times of the day, what needs to be accomplished but, we do not know how it will all turn out... your today is a blank page. Get up willing to seize the day, 'carpe diem!' Start with a positive attitude that everything will work out fabulous! Start your children's day with the same attitude! Put on some music in the morning, music that inspires you, builds you up and puts a smile on your face. Take that smile with you for the rest of the day, and you will be amazed how that changes your disposition, and creates positive outcomes to everything you touch.

At night, take a moment to reflect on your day. Have a conversation with yourself and ask, what went really well and better than expected today? What can you do tomorrow that will make your day even better? What changes can you implement to take your next day to a new level? Foster a habit of positive thinking and believing, and watch your life and your children's life soar! And... be grateful...

Believe in yourself. You've got this parenting thing. You already have the knowledge and wisdom to raise incredible human beings...

Love yourself. Stay positive.

Empowerment through Effective Communication

"Empowering communication systems will improve the ability
To withstand disasters."
—Andrew Lippman

Give your child the understanding of how much power they have in controlling their destiny. One of the first things we can do is teach them good communication, and how to use their voice.

As an example, when my son was young, he played on a soccer team and his coach was his best friend's father. My son's father, through the enjoyment of my son's sport, liked to try and help our son by telling him where to run to, and to get someone to check, and to run there. On the other hand, the coach was also giving instructions, and for a while my son would be upset and confused about this. We sat down and talked about how he was feeling.

Now, my son when he was young had a big heart and never wanted to hurt anyone for any reason. In our discussions, he said that he didn't like it when Dad yelled at him and told him where to go on the field, and then the coach would yell at him and tell him to do something different. He felt like he needed to please both, but he didn't know how.

When he told me how he was feeling, this was a time I could help empower him to handle some of these life situations, and teach him how to deal with them himself. I told him he really needs to express this thoughts to his Dad and ask him not to say anything anymore from the sidelines because it is confusing to him. I also told him that because it was his own feelings, he needed to be the one to have the conversation with his dad, and not have me tell his dad for him. I also told him we could practice what he wanted to say together, I could pretend I was his dad, and he could practice telling me so he could do this on his own, and feel confident. So, we practiced and we practiced. I also told him he needed to decide when to do this, I was not going to make him do it, it was completely in his control.

A number of weeks went by and each week, he still expressed to me he didn't like both his dad and the coach telling him what to do. I reminded him that he has the power to talk to his dad, then I also told him, he has permission to talk to his dad and sort it out so he felt better. Somehow, I think when I gave him permission, it also made it easier for my son to approach his father. I believe he felt I had his back in a different way, and he needed that.

> *"A lot of people are afraid to say what they want, that's why they don't get what they want."* —Madonna

Finally, after a soccer game, my son went to his dad and said, "Dad, I need to tell you that I don't like it when you yell and tell me what to do on the field. I really just want to listen to my coach and do what he tells me so I don't get confused." His dad had not realized he was causing confusion, he was only caught in the excitement of watching his son play soccer. He apologized and said, "absolutely, from now on listen to your coach!"

It was handled and done and no longer did my son struggle with trying to please both the coach and his father. He learned that he has a voice and can speak up and stick up for what he believes. He had the control to decide when it was best for him to do this, and the whole experience was a lesson in empowerment. This was so much better than me going to ask his father not to do it anymore.

Take life situations and turn them into opportunities for your child, teach them and walk them through, rehearse with them if they need to and explain the up side and the down side of how things can go but, most important, let them handle their own issues as much as possible.

> *"You can only go forward by making mistakes."* —Alexander McQueen

When my son was young, he would be so hard on himself, he was a bit of a perfectionist, had a hard time living up to his own expectations and felt like he made too many mistakes. One day, his frustration with himself not being perfect was so wearing on me, I knew I needed to deal with this subject so he didn't have to live his life not feeling like enough, and terrorized by making mistakes.

This one day, I took a look at what he was trying to accomplish. I had to sit him down and ask him why he felt he needed to do it perfectly. Although I don't recall now what he said, I do remember asking him to quickly see if he had a belly button, it was urgent that he find it! He found his belly button and said, "Yes, I have one Mom!" I breathed a huge sigh of relief. He has a belly button! I asked him if he knew what that meant as this is a big and powerful find! He said he didn't know! I said with relief, "If you are lucky enough to find a belly button that can only mean one thing, it means it is expected that what you do does not have to be perfect, just your best. It also means you are expected to make mistakes and learn from them!" This was wonderful news! He quickly asked if I had one too, and as it turned out I did! Having a belly button makes you 'human' and being human means that everyone with a belly button makes mistakes and is not perfect! Quite joyous news wouldn't you agree?

With that, I saw him relax a little while the news sunk in. It was a great moment. Once we realize that it is okay, and actually give ourselves permission to make mistakes, it can seriously reduce stress levels, and it is empowering.

GUILT AND SHAME
AND THE NAME GAME

"Guilt = I did something bad.
Shame = I am bad.
Shame is about who we are, and guilt is about your behaviours."
—Brene Brown

Guilt and Shame are tactics that many parents use to control and manipulate their children into doing and behaving a certain way. Guilt and shame are separators. Where there is guilt and/ or shame, there cannot be love. Where there is jealousy and/ or envy, there cannot be love. Where there is competition in a relationship, there cannot be love. When we are to love our child unconditionally, guilt and shame cannot be involved.

There are people out there that we do not know, their name is 'society' and they can tend to dictate how we should raise our children. 'Society says we should or shouldn't do the following.' From breast feeding to discipline, society has an opinion on our lives. So I ask, who is society anyway and what do they know about my life and my children? What makes them right and me wrong?

What about, rather than having society tell me how to raise my children and pre-determine what I should or shouldn't do, and make us feel guilty and shameful for our choices, what if instead... we got to know our children through communication, ask our children their thoughts, listen and understand our children so we know what they as individuals are capable of, and let the parents determine what is right or wrong for their children.

I am personally familiar with being made to feel guilt and shame at a time when I didn't fully understand that I didn't need to take it on. Taking it on stunted my growth emotionally. All of us I am sure, have been made to feel guilty and shamed at one time or another, and I don't know of a single person that would say they enjoyed that feeling.

> *"Shame is the lie someone told you about yourself."* —Anais Nin

Many of us are hard enough on ourselves that we don't need to be made to feel guilt on top of it all. To manipulate a child is fundamentally wrong, and all it will do is teach the child that it is how they get things in life, through the art of manipulation and guilt. Should you expose your child to this young, do not be surprised when your child does it back to you in their teens. When they do, the parent will be appalled and even stunned. It is not the child's fault, it was taught to them, and they are only doing what their parents did to them. The blame lies in the parent.

Many times, this takes the form of belittling or calling their own children names or labeling them in a negative way. In observing the art of shame, I have also observed the child and their reaction to this.

Have you ever thought about what is in a name? There can be plenty and both positive and negative. These names we are called are names that consciously or subconsciously we tend to navigate towards, and actually become, because we embrace them into our perception of ourselves simply because other people use this name for us. There are also sweet, fun hearted and loving nicknames which are adoring and positive however, I would like to focus on the ones to avoid and be aware of.

> *"Nicknames are potent ways of cutting people down to size."* —Doris Lessing

Personally, as a young child I was given the name or label, 'stupid.' I was called this because I was simply someone that liked to take their time. I was late often in my childhood, although it was outgrown. I was also a slow eater and was sometimes slow to make a decision. It had nothing to do with my IQ, however, because I was called this so often, I came to believe this label.

This label and my belief of it, contributed to holding me back in my life choices. Because of believing I was stupid, I didn't have the confidence to voice my opinion, as I was convinced that what I had to say would be stupid. I internalized this label.

When I finished high school and got a job, I was doing small claims for a company, and the companies lawyer came to me one day and said I did great work and if I was interested in pursuing a career as a lawyer, he would be happy to help me through. I was stunned by the offer but quickly declined it because I just didn't think or believe I was smart enough to go to university. This self-limiting belief was so powerful, it made me not believe in myself. Although I graduated from high school, got every job I applied for, and even became the first female in a management role for a large company at the age of nineteen, I still felt and believed in my core that I wasn't smart enough.

Later in life when my kids were young, I took a course in Counselling and received honours from a distance education university. It took until this time for me to start fully believing in myself, and let the label go, and started living my life in my new reality. I do wonder what life may have been like for me had I been raised with confidence in myself rather than the negative labels.

> *"Children become what they are told they are."* —Dorothy Delay

When I raised my children, I was very aware of these labels and how toxic they are, and decided the only label I would give my children if any, was going to be something positive. Parental control that is not widely talked about is the ability to merge your child with great outcomes, and this is powerful. If you label your child something negative, once the child buys into that name, they will subconsciously live up to that name. The parent is responsible for this, and therefore I recommend you choose wisely.

A child that grows up always being call a 'brat' has a likelihood of about ninety per cent of being a brat. A child being called a clown will likely become the 'class clown.' We subconsciously live up to our label, and when it does damage to another person, we just blame the label. Such as, I made a stupid decision but, I am stupid so why expect anything less or more? Again, in these examples you can input any name, and have the same results. Unfortunately for many, this is not an easy movement to change this belief.

So, knowing that what you put into your child is what you will get, wouldn't you love your child enough to label them something that is positive and that will work in their life to empower them? I gave my daughter the name of 'wise one' and she was and still is, more wise than a lifetime should make a person. My son received the name of 'hero' and in every sense of the word, he was, and continues to be, my greatest hero.

Did you have a label as a child? How did it work for you? Make sure you carefully consider that a simple name can have a powerful and life lasting impact on your child.

> *"You can talk bad about me all you want. But if you say something to hurt my child... not even God can save you."* —A Mom's Life, Uncut

I have watched other parents say negative names to their child, and at times I have been stunned by the child's reaction. One day I said to an acquaintance's daughter, "Wow, you are so beautiful and I love your hair!" The little girl replied with, "No, I'm not, I'm fat." The parent said, "Yes you are a little porker." I simply felt sick and didn't know what to say, this little girl was only about ten. Another young girl I know was also called fat at school, and she took it on personally and became anorexic for which the entire family suffered, but the good news is that she did get the help she needed to recover.

These names we think nothing about when we carelessly put them out there, thinking they are cute when they are very small, these names will grow with the child. Make sure it is a name that will empower them to do great and be great. Just to clarify, using derogatory names on your child for the purpose of trying to keep them humble, does not work, it actually destroys.

Making comparisons between your child and other children and pointing out how someone else can do things so much better, also destroys self-esteem. Making them feel guilty because they didn't complete a task as well as another or shaming them over it, can stunt their emotional growth and the damage can be deep and last a lifetime.

What about yourself at work, you have a busy day and think you have handled it well, only to realize before going to bed that you forgot or missed something very important. Something you knew should have been done and have no excuse for it. You get stressed, upset, frustrated because it was simple and you knew it needed to be done. You feel shame because you knew better but just didn't do better. I trust this is not a pleasant feeling for you and it's even worse for a child.

In life, things happen out of our control. We should prepare our children for disappointment and teach them how to deal with it themselves, and how to find a way to pick themselves up again.

If someone is treating you with guilt and shame, we can choose not to accept it. We need to realize this is purely the thoughts and feelings of someone else, thoughts and feelings that don't belong to us, and we are not responsible for them.

There should be no guilt or shame, just acceptance of our circumstance. If as a parent you accuse your child of making you feel angry, and then make them feel guilty of it, you are hurting your child. It is similar to bullying and it is a form of abuse. Manipulating your children is also a form of abuse. It only hurts and destroys self-esteem, and puts a wedge in your relationship.

Using these techniques to have your children do what you want them to do, is not parenting, it does nothing for your relationship with the child, except create alienation. If you find yourself slipping into this deception, and can identify why, please go to your child and apologize and explain what was happening to you to make you say or do those things to your child. Your goal is to prevent your child from using those methods that ultimately will destroy your relationship.

> *"What counts is not just that we believe we love them unconditionally, but that they feel loved in that way."* —Alfie Kohn

Our love for our children is meant to be unconditional. When we use guilt and shame to manipulate a child, we are also sending a message to them that as long as you do what I want you to, how I want you to do it, then I will love you. I can only wish you good luck with that, as you will need a great deal of help when this child is in their teens and beyond. The child may turn out okay, however your relationship is not going to be as close as it could have been.

PUNISHMENT AND DISCIPLINE

"We need to understand the difference
between discipline and punishment.
Punishment is what you do to *someone;*
Discipline is what you do for *someone."*
—Zig Ziglar

Punishment and discipline have two very different and distinct meanings and quite often I witness parents using both inter-changeably, believing they have the same meaning.

Punishment is to cause a person to pay for a fault. Discipline is a strict training of mind or character. They really are nothing alike.

Where do we get our resources from regarding punishment and discipline? It is passed down from generation to generation? How was yours as a child and how do you think it worked? Perhaps you think it was good because after all, you turned out well and that is good enough. For others, was anything missing or, as you look back now, do you wish it was done a different way?

As you can see by the definitions above, these words are very different and yet they are used the same way in the minds of many parents. Just by looking at the definition, can you tell what the difference would be in your child by what method you choose to use?

> *"When we use punishment, our children are robbed of the opportunity to develop their own inner discipline—the ability to act with integrity, wisdom, compassion, and mercy when there is no external force holding them accountable for what they do."* —Barbara Coloroso

We want to raise a generation of well adjusted, responsible, authentic, self-respecting individuals and by choosing punishment, we can cause some emotional damage to our child.

When your child does something wrong, (and I am referring to the usual growing up issues here, and not the severe issues that require intervention), do you want your child to grow from learning their lesson or, do you want your child to pay for their mistake?

Paying for a mistake seems harsh and out of line, making mistakes is part of life and growing. It infers the child will be put to shame, embarrassment, and the message the child receives about themselves is, they are not enough, not good enough, and their opinion of themselves plummits. Is that what you want your child to feel? Think about the future of this child that has been held to punishment. Just as saying the word 'no' too often, the child becomes immune to the word, so does a child about being punished regularly, they also become immune. There is a chance when they get older they won't care about consequences as this is really all they know – punishment.

Let's look at putting a child into a corner to think about what they have done. At the time my children were young, this was a popular way of punishing a young child for doing something wrong. Let's think about that. A young child put into a corner... alone... to think about what they have done. What is the purpose of this really? Do we think a young child will come out of the corner enlightened, apologetic, and a better child? The child is likely in the corner thinking about how they could have used a different colour crayon on the wall, and how pretty it looked, and why didn't everyone like it as much as them? Now they feel shame, are lonely, and isolated.

> *"The more disciplined you become, the easier life gets."* —Vishwas Chavan

If you want your child to practice discipline, it is important for the parent to be an example of discipline. Remember at the beginning of the book I wrote, 'Do not ask your child to do anything that you yourself cannot do.' Discipline also applies to the parent. Parents need to have consistent training of the mind and character, we want to empower our children. In simple terms, if we say 'no,' we need to stick to it and be consistent, this demonstrating parental discipline. If we ask our children to do something and they do another thing, we need to be consistent about training their mind to do the right thing. Using positive, consistent discipline, parents help to develop their character, their conscious thought, their ability to feel remorse, and it's important not to bury your children in self-pity.

For example, the child colours on the wall, we take away the crayons, look at our child and explain that that was incorrect behaviour and why. Talk to your child so they know they can do great artwork on art paper but, to do it on the walls in the family home is not a good idea. Have your child help you clean it up and after they do, it is likely they will learn from that experience and not do it again. You have taught them with an explanation of what was wrong, and you are still loving your child. This is empowerment. Remember, this child has not lived as long as you, and it is in their mandate to do things wrong, that is how they learn.

> *"Patience is not the ability to wait, but the ability to keep a good attitude while waiting."* —Unknown

This method of discipline takes patience. If you have lost your patience… you need to stop now, and go find it. It is not a mere suggestion, it is a requirement and one quality that can save you great and unnecessary frustration.

One thing I want to point out is that it is always important to refer to their 'behaviour' as bad and not the 'child' is bad. It is not personal, and the child is not bad, the behaviour was.

—— Choose to Share the Joy… ——

"There is no joy in life
Like the joy of sharing."
—Billy Graham

There was a time I heard a father yell at his daughter who was just sixteen. Apparently, she had found a car that was perfect for her and her new driver's licence. She called her father to let him know the wonderful news, and he blew up at her because he had said that now is not a good time for him to help her buy a car, and they had agreed to the spring. She was crushed and said, "No wonder I don't tell you anything, you can never be nice."

Later, I talked to the father and I asked him why he yelled at her. He said, "Because she knew I said the car would be in the spring." I suggested another way of thinking. I enlightened him to the fact that she is only sixteen with a new driver's licence, of course she is over the moon with excitement, and reminded him this moment will never come again in her lifetime. This is a first step into adulthood, responsibility, freedom and a very pivotal time in a child's life. Why not take a moment and just share the joy with your daughter? Get excited with her about the car and listen to how excited she is. Ask her to sit down afterwards, and then you can remind her of your agreement that was made previously, and the importance of sticking to the original plan. There will be another perfect car for her when you are both ready, and in the meantime, you can share some good times looking around together.

As this is a special time in every teen's life, why not create a memory for them of a special time? Every time this girl looks back on turning sixteen and getting her first car, she will have negative thoughts because all she will remember is her father yelling at her. This only happens one time, you only have one very first car, there is not a do-over, at a later time. There will be many special 'one-time' only moments in your child's life. Choose to make them truly special and memorable.

This story is about a father wanting to punish his daughter for being excited about buying a car without his input. Remember back to when you were getting your first car and the excitement, how would you have wanted your father or mother to react in this situation? How do you think his relationship with his daughter would change, if he took the time to share the joy first?

Parental Discipline

"Discipline is doing what needs to be done,
Even if you don't want to do it."
—Carolyn Hansen

Another example is of a mother and her teenage daughter. The young girl was angry at her mother because she was not given permission to go out and do what she wanted. This girl ran to my house and said, she hated her mom and her mom didn't understand. She wanted to be with her friends and her mother was ruining her life. It was a bit extreme but, in the moment, it was a big deal to her.

The girl's mom called me and said, "Please talk to my daughter for me, I am at my wit's end and don't know what to do." Normally, I don't get too involved but, I agreed to talk to her daughter and told the mom what I would be saying to her daughter, so everything was up front.

"Acknowledgement is the only way to keep love alive." —Barry Long

I sat down with this girl and said, "You are angry at your mom, eh?" She said yes, and she hated her mom and didn't ever want to go home. "My mom doesn't understand me." I let her vent her frustration and she talked for about fifteen minutes. It is important to let them get out their feelings, don't let your child keep their feelings bottled up. Expression is healthy. I looked at her and was very present while she talked, she needed to be heard and validated. Only at this point can you move forward to make your point, otherwise it ends up in no one listening to one another, and nothing gets solved. Once she has been heard, she has no choice but to listen in return.

I then told her that I completely understand what she is saying and how she feels. Acknowledgement of their feelings is necessary. I told her that I remember feeling just like her when I was her age. I'm sure we can all recall a memory similar to this in our own childhood. Then I had her attention and I could begin teaching her about the parental role, and how not giving in means discipline, and much love.

I explained to her that in fact, her mom was doing exactly what she should be doing, and it is only out of love and partly fear, that she decided she would not allow her to go off and do what she pleased. In order for her to truly understand, I used a story, and put her in a role in that story.

I said, "You have done a lot of babysitting am I right? While you are babysitting, you have a responsibility to keep the child safe, correct? What if you didn't do anything except listen to music, watch TV and the toddler did what she pleased. Would that be acceptable?" Obviously, her answer was no. I said, "What if, the stove was on, and the toddler was walking towards it with their hand out, what would you do?"

She replied, "Well of course I would stop her."

I asked her why. She looked at me with a 'well duh' expression and said, "Because she would burn or hurt herself."

I smiled and replied, "Exactly. You would be doing what is expected of you in a position of caring for another person. Your mom also has a responsibility to keep you safe, and maybe she said no because she could see that you were heading for danger and her fear jumped in because, she doesn't want anything to happen to you and she doesn't want you hurt because, she loves you very much."

I waited and watched her face, and I could see the light come on. I explained the last thing her mom wanted was to ruin her social life, that was not her intention. Her intention is only to protect her, and that my dear is pure love, nothing less. I then asked if she still hated her mom. She was embarrassed and said no, she was just sad now that she couldn't go out with her friends but, now she understood why.

She went home to her mom and later that night, her mom called me and said, "I don't know what you said but I owe you big time. She came home, walked into the house and came up to me and gave me a hug, apologized and then she told me she loves me. My daughter has never done this and it put me to tears."

I was so happy to hear this and it was a new beginning for this mother and daughter. I told her mom, never be afraid to talk to your child and explain how you feel, as well as listen and relate to them, treat your child how you would want to be treated.

> *"Where did we ever get the crazy idea that in order to make children do better, first we have to make them feel worse? Think of the last time you felt humiliated or treated unfairly. Did you feel like cooperating or doing better?"*
> —Jane Nelsen

At the end of the day, does punishment or discipline serve your child better now and in their future? If a child is 'punished' in their childhood for all the things they do wrong, they become conditioned to this type of penalty. The child grows up knowing if they do something wrong, they will have to serve their time by way of a grounding, standing in a corner or being spanked or some negative form of 'paying the price.' This becomes their 'normal,' it becomes expected and the impact of this becomes less and less. When they get to be a teen and their actions are more serious, they don't develop remorse or fear of police, juvenile houses, even court or jail. To them, it is expected and conditioned into them, and they know they just have to serve their time, and then life will move on.

The Marble Jar

"Your beliefs don't make you a better person;
Your behaviour does…"
—Sukhraj Dhillon

When my children were very little I brought out a marble jar. This is just a masonry jar, and a bag of marbles. I set out to teach behaviour. I did not want to spend their childhood yelling at them about behaving properly, all yelling to your child does is teach them to yell back. Not helpful.

Each of my children had their own jar, and I asked them to find a picture of something they really wanted. When they found the picture, I asked them why they chose what they did so I would know how important it was to them. If it wasn't something important to them, I would ask them to choose again. We will not work toward something if it is not important to us.

Once they had the picture, I taped it to the outside of the jar. I explained they could have what they have chosen, when the marble jar was full, and not until then. In order for the jar to get filled, they could earn marbles by doing good things. They could earn marbles for being kind and sharing between the two of them, they could earn marbles for cleaning up their toys when asked the first time to do so. You as the parent can put in place the behaviours that you want your child to have. For each time they did something well, the bag of marbles would be opened, and the child would put their hand in and take out the parents determined amount of marbles they had earned, and put it in the jar themselves. This way, they have some responsibility and they feel good, it gives them more control, and we are all about building self-esteem.

I told my kids they can earn marbles as quickly as they would like. It was in their control. The other side was if they did something with a negative behaviour, like not sharing with their sibling or not cleaning up after the first time asked, the marble bag would be opened again but this time, the child would put their hand in the marble jar and remove the amount of marbles determined by the parent, and put them back into the marble bag to be re-earned later. This also teaches your child to take responsibility, and it is a better lesson when they take them out themselves.

Remember to talk to your child about their good behaviour, to be excited and pleased and say thank you to your child. When they are removing marbles, do the same and talk to them about the behaviour that warranted the removal, why it was not good and how they can avoid that behaviour going forward.

When the child fills the jar, make good on your promise to get what they have chosen. Get only what they chose and nothing else. It is very important that we don't go overboard, we only want to get what they chose so they see the reward, and they keep control of this lesson.

> *"With self-discipline most anything is possible."* —Theodore Roosevelt

It may sound a bit odd but, because I used discipline and started when my children were young, I never instituted a list of rules for them to follow. Through teaching what is expected, their level of demonstrated behaviour showed me what they were capable of and boundaries were set accordingly.

If a child is taught by discipline, this will serve them far better over the course of their life. It means a little more work on the parents' side but really, you are teaching them a life skill that will benefit them now, and all through their life. It will make the teen years much easier. With discipline they learn a behaviour, a behaviour that will work for them when they go to school and understand they need self-discipline to get their homework done, and they will need discipline to do a good job out in the workforce.

TRUST AND BROKEN PROMISES

"People ask me why it's so hard to trust people,
and I ask them why is it so hard to keep a promise."
—Amy Rees Anderson

Relationships cannot be sustained without trust between the people in the relationship. The word 'trust' is to believe, the word 'promise' is a pledge that one will or will not do something and the word 'broken' means incomplete, weak and crushed.

This book is about raising children, and from that perspective, if you always told your kids what was true, they learn to depend and trust what you say, as long as you follow up with what you said you were going to do. I just want you to open your mind to this thought. In parenting, we tell our children to tell the truth so that we can trust them. This also holds true for parents, we must tell the truth to be trusted by our children.

Trust is paramount in your parent-child relationship. Teach your child what it means to trust, what the behaviours are and why it is so important. Start this young because as the child grows and your trust between each of you grows, this will develop a bonding relationship.

"Trust Children. Nothing could be more simple—or more difficult. Difficult, because to trust children, we must trust ourselves. And most of us were taught as children that we could not be trusted." —John Holt

One of the first times my kids went out on their own was to walk to the corner store. We went over their route to the store and how I was trusting them not to deviate from that route, just in case something happened, and the rule was they had to stay together. They were about eight and ten, and I remember watching them walk down the street until they turned the corner, and were out of sight. I did not like the feeling but knew I also had to grow up and let them go. After a ridiculous amount of pacing back and forth, eventually I saw their happy little faces turn the corner and I let out a breath I wasn't even aware I had been holding.

Because this went well, we started moving toward some independence as they had earned my trust and earned the chance to experience some freedom. As long as when they ventured out, they called me to let me know they got where they were going, the trust and freedom door opened a little more each time.

There are going to be times that a parent doesn't tell the full truth to protect the child and in most cases, this can be acceptable. Where it is not acceptable is when we are reacting out of anger and say something like, if they continue with that behaviour you will break their arm. This is not true, but sometimes we say things without thinking them through. Stop and breathe … then act, not react.

If our intention is never to really break the child's arm, then why say it? We will have much more success by saying, if they continue that behaviour they will be sent to bed, or there will be no snack, or they will not be able to watch TV, something that we can follow through on.

Broken Promises

"Trust is important
But once a promise is broken,
Sorry means nothing."
—Drake

I would like you to think of a time when you had plans to do something that was very exciting, and you had prepared for it mentally and physically. A time that you had looked forward to as, a moment to remember. It was all planned and perhaps you were so excited you lived the event in your head for weeks, and it made you smile every time you thought about it. Now hold onto that thought …

The time finally arrives, and suddenly you learn that it is not going to happen, not at all. No explanations are given to you, the moment that was to take place, just came… and went. Nothing, just … nothing. How are you feeling? Sad, disappointed, angry, lost, empty, afraid, let down, untrusting …

When a parent breaks a promise to a child, that is what they are feeling and not to mention, this is a lot of feelings for a young child who hasn't lived through these thoughts and feelings before. As a parent, we can identify with our own thoughts through our life experiences. Our life experiences have taught us and we learned to cope with disappointment however, our child has not had that luxury, and now does not know what to do with all those feelings. Because they are confused and feeling so many things, many children will release them by acting out, getting aggressive, and not fully understanding why they are behaving in this manner.

Now, sometimes we are going to tell our children that we will do something and because of life circumstances, it doesn't end up happening. In this case we need to teach our children this is a reality of life, we cannot always get what we want. We need to teach our children to bounce back emotionally. We need to explain what took place that put our plans on hold. It is about being flexible and compromising. Making a promise that you cannot keep is essentially, lying to your child to appease them at that moment. Be aware of the damage that can do.

We ask our children to promise to be good, and ask them to make all kinds of promises to us, and when they don't follow through, the parent usually ends up angry and reminding the child they promised. If the parent breaks their promises, isn't the child doing exactly what the parent is doing? *We* need to be the example so our children learn the value of a promise or, of keeping our word and their word.

> *"Commitment means staying loyal to what you said you were going to do long after the mood you said it in has left you."* —Master Jonathan Field

By keeping our promises, we build trust and security. The child has the security of knowing they can trust what the parent is telling them. The same goes the other way, we need to be the example so that when our child promises to be good, we believe their word. Building this trust takes time and consistency, not to mention patience. If you want to promise your child something but, you are not sure if it will actually materialize, then say to them, we will make this plan but there are other circumstances that can come into play that may prevent it from happening so, I will do my best however, I cannot make a promise on this right now. It is okay to do this.

APOLOGIZE AND FORGIVE

"When a person tells you that you hurt them,
you don't get to decide that you didn't."
—Louis C.K.

There is a great saying from whom I do not know, and it goes something like this. Take a plate and hold it. Now drop that plate on the floor. What happens? The plate breaks into pieces. Now, say sorry to the plate. Does it go back together? No. Now think of your child's feelings, as the plate.

There will be many times during your child-raising years that things happen or get said that hurt either the child or the parent. There will be times as a parent that you just want to give up and quit your parenting role, as it is so difficult. Know that you are not alone.

> *"Apologizing does not always mean that you're wrong and the other person is right. It just means that you value your relationship more than your ego."* —Mark Matthews

As important as teaching your child to say 'please,' and 'thank you,' so is teaching them how to apologize, and also for you to learn to apologize to your child. As parents, we will make mistakes too from time to time, and it is important for us to set an example for our children.

There may be a time that you accidentally close the door on your child's fingers, your adrenaline rushes and you grab your child and say sorry ninety-two times while kissing the precious little fingers. It was an accident, and your intention was not to hurt your child, and the realization that you did, likely hurts the parents far more than the child's fingers. With the same depth of your 'I'm sorry' in this situation, is how the words 'I'm sorry' should be said, every time.

> *"I'm sorry that my forced apology sounded insincere, I will try to make it more convincing next time."* —Unknown

Do you remember in your childhood, a parent or an elder telling you to say you were sorry and, because you were mad at the time you just harshly said the words? There really was no – or very little – remorse or emotion in the words, they were just words, you didn't mean them, you only said them because you were told to.

The person that you were saying sorry to really doesn't pick up the feeling that you meant those words, and nothing gets fixed or better, and the fight continues.

We want to teach our children, that saying sorry and apologizing are said with true emotion, and only when you really mean the words you are speaking. We also need to learn how to get to this place when we are angry. When an apology is said with sincerity and is meant from the heart, this is the glue that mends brokenness. This is an opportunity to move past the issue and have closure. That is why we want to say it like you would have, having just closed the door on little fingers.

> *"Never ruin an apology with an excuse."*
> —Benjamin Franklin

For an apology to have the right effect, it should be said with more words than just, I'm sorry. There should be a 'what' you are sorry about and an acknowledgement for the other person's feelings. Such as, "I am so very sorry that I called you that name, and hurt your feelings. It wasn't very nice of me, and I feel bad for saying it, please forgive me ..." These words or words like them, will help in mending what is broken. When we acknowledge another's feelings, that is when the healing can begin. If we fail to do this, the person we are apologizing to does not feel validated. In order for that person to move forward and forgive, there needs to be validation.

As parents, it is important that we do not view our title of parent as not having faults or being above apologizing to our children. Children learn from our behaviours, and if we want them to apologize for what they do, we must also apologize for what we do. It is not up to us to judge what hurts another, as said before, we are all different. Would you like someone to tell you that your feelings are wrong and therefore they won't apologize? We don't have to agree with the other person, but if you see that your child's feelings are hurt, we must do something to mend those broken feelings so that we all can move on and forward.

Forgiveness

"If we really want to love,
We must learn how to forgive."
—Mother Teresa

When faced with the knowledge we need to forgive, many will ignore it instead of face it. For whatever reason, many believe if they forgive, the other wins. It is not about winning or loosing or who is right and who is wrong. Because of this I want to make it very clear just what Forgiveness is. It is about releasing the bitterness. We cannot control others, only ourselves.

Let's begin with the Wikipedia meaning...

"Forgiveness is the intentional and voluntary process by which a victim undergoes a change in feelings and attitude regarding an offence, lets go of negative emotions such as vengefulness, with an increased ability to wish the offender well."

If your life has not already provided you with situations that need forgiveness, consider yourself blessed. However, for the majority of us, we have all had things happen that require our forgiveness or we simply chose to hang on to the bitterness like a warm blanket. The deceiving part is that hanging on to it, does not give us any comfort or peace.

Think of it in these terms. Recall the first time someone said or did something to hurt your feelings. Now, imagine a winter jacket representing the hurt you are hanging on to. Put the jacket on. Now recall another time someone hurt you... put on another jacket over the first one. Again, remember another hurt... put on another jacket on top of the second jacket. How are you feeling? Weighed down? Like you can't move properly?

132 — B. Janine Fulla

Suffocating? Does it also make you feel angry that it is holding you back from moving freely?

> *"Forgiveness is not an occasional act, it is a constant attitude."* —Rev Martin Luther King, Jr.

In reality, this is what you are doing to yourself by holding on, not releasing, and not forgiving. There is not one thing positive that hanging on to this is going to give you, not one positive thing. It is not 'strong' to hang on to it, in fact it is a 'weak' choice. Get strong… release!

Now, in your mind, light a nice marshmallow roasting fire. Remove the top jacket and toss it in the fire, and tell yourself how much you *don't need* it. Now, remove the next jacket, toss it on the fire and tell yourself how much you *don't want* it. Now remove the last jacket, toss it on the fire and realize how good the freedom feels! Feel the release, feel the lightness, feel the breeze on your skin! You are FREE!

Why would you choose to hold on to all those layers of weight? Do you think the person that hurt you cares how much weight you were holding, and how confined you were? Nope, they don't. They have gotten on with their own life and forgotten about yours. So, this sounds like the only one that is still hurting is yourself, and it's only because you are choosing to. It's kind of silly, wouldn't you agree, and of no value to you.

If you have issues in your life now, perhaps someone did or said something to hurt you, and you told yourself, 'I will never forgive you,' remember you are the only one suffering by this. Not forgiving does not give you power, it gives the power to the person that hurt you! Why would you do that?

> *"Forgiveness doesn't excuse their behaviour. Forgiveness prevents their behaviour from destroying your heart."* —Unknown

Teach your children to forgive by being an example. Life is full of burdens and issues and hurts. The sooner we learn to get over it, and on with it, the better and more powerful our lives will be.

TAKING RESPONSIBILITY

"It is easy to dodge responsibilities but
we cannot dodge the consequences of dodging responsibilities."
—Josiah Charles Stamp

Taking responsibility is the state or act of being answerable or accountable. This can be viewed by the parent in the form of being responsible for the child's safety, health, food and shelter, which are all true and very important. These are things that as parents we tend to handle, as they are life's basics. I want to go further with responsibility.

— Parents are Responsible for Environment —

"On a positive note, we must reaffirm the right of children
To grow up in a family with a father and mother capable
Of creating a suitable environment for
The child's development and emotional maturity."
—Pope Francis

As parents, we need to be responsible for our own actions and behaviours. If we are unaware of what we as parents are putting out in our environment, the children can be the ones to suffer.

Some homes are filled with yelling, arguing, bitterness and resentment. Some are filled with jealousy and control. It is the parent's responsibility to be aware of the environment. Both adults and children will be a product of your environment. If all children see is fighting and yelling, the child will grow up believing this is okay and quite normal. The children will live their life in the same way, as they won't know differently. If a child grows up in a home full of jealousy and control, the child will be jealous and controlling. Later in the big world when they are grown and are living their life in this manner, finding rejection, they may not fully understand why. We need to be conscious of what we, the parents are putting into our environment.

As a parent of young children that have play dates, be responsible and get to know your children's friends and their families. Know the environment they are going to play in, don't assume and judge another family before getting to know them. Volunteer at your children's school and get to know the parents and other children. When my daughter was in elementary school, there were only a few girls that my daughter clicked with, and out of that few, there were only a couple that we trusted her going to their house after school to play. We did not have great reviews on some of the families of the friends she had, so we made a decision to put her in another school, for her last year of elementary school. This turned out to be the best choice, as she quickly made friends with children from great homes and they remain best friends even today.

Sometimes, we need to take responsibility for our children's environment to the degree of making some large changes, and sacrifices to ensure our children have a good opportunity.

————— Responsibility Lessons —————

"It is not only for what we do that we are held responsible, but also for what we do not do."
—Moliere

The responsibility as a parent lies in what lessons we choose to teach our children. I shall admit that I did not excel at teaching my children to clean their room or to cook. It was somewhat deliberate, as I realized I have only so many opportunities to teach something and I chose to teach life and emotional well-being. I reasoned that they will learn eventually to clean their mess, wash their clothes, and I know they will not starve. I chose this because I also did not want to fight with my child about the condition of their room vs. their personal character. When I released them into the world, I wanted to know that I am releasing good people. The world doesn't care if their room is clean and to me, that is why there was a door on their room. Not saying this isn't important, just pick your battles.

Taking responsibility or being accountable in my home was a must. Again, this can be taught at a very young age.

When my son was quite young, he and his sister were playing and he ended up breaking one of my CD's. He disappeared for a bit. When he came back, he was emotionally upset and told me to go look at my bed. It didn't make sense to me but, I followed his direction as he seemed upset by something I was unaware of. I went to my room and on my bed, my son had placed the broken CD, a note with a written apology, and the money to replace the CD.

My child took responsibility because he was taught how to and the meaning of it. I was so touched by what he had done and was so happy to realize the lesson had gotten through to him. Sometimes when we teach our children lessons, it can take years to really know if the lesson was received.

> *"The ultimate step in taking responsibility is making sure our actions line up with our words."* —John C. Maxwell

I always told my children that if they took responsibility for their actions, were sincerely sorry, and told the truth, that I would not be upset with them, nor yell at them. So, now it was my turn to remember my promise and not get upset about a broken CD. It wasn't about the CD, it was about the actions my son took. I was so proud of him and told him so. I hugged him and said, "Thank you for taking responsibility as I know it is sometimes not easy to do." I told him that he is growing up, and that he had just made my trust for him grow by ten times.

It is important when we see our child do something good, that they be rewarded with positive feedback, and in most cases, giving this positive feedback is more helpful to our child than buying an item or candy, etc. This way we are cultivating a behaviour that we want to see more of. If I were to react and get mad about the broken CD, the child would see no value in taking responsibility because they would just get yelled at, so why bother. Check yourself as the parent and make sure your reaction is the proper reaction to create more of this good behaviour.

—— Think Carefully Before You React ——

"Before you act, Listen!
Before you react, Think!"
—Ernest Hemmingway

When my daughter was just fourteen, I was in her room and found a bottle of alcohol in her knapsack. I was stunned. I confronted her after I took some time to think about how I wanted this conversation to go. I would not accept that it belonged to her friend, and she was only holding on to it for them. I think we have all used that one when we were children. I wanted to position the conversation so that she would tell the truth, and take responsibility for her actions.

When I spoke with her, I didn't freak out, yell and scream. If I had done that, she would have gotten on her defensive clothes and the outcome would not have been good. When thinking about my approach, it was important for me to remember that when I was her age, I did a similar thing. I thought if it were me, how would I like my parents to talk to me, then I proceeded.

"If you want children to keep their feet on the ground, put some responsibility on their shoulders." —Abigail Van Buren

I asked her about the alcohol calmly but, with a sense of disappointment as I didn't want her to think this was okay. She did own up to it, that it was hers, and told me what was happening. This would not have taken place had we not developed our communication when she was little. I kept my cool even if on the inside I was freaking out a little. When it came to responsibility, I told her that her dad would not be pleased about this. Having said that, I told her that if she was responsible enough to make this choice that wasn't good, she was responsible enough to tell her dad the truth, and that I would not tell him to smooth things over. She then had to tell her dad herself and accept what was coming, that is the joy of making decisions and dealing with the responsibility and consequences.

My daughter was not a victim in her decision. She owned her actions and we don't want our children to play the part of the victim and blame others for their own actions, and mistakes. She needed to be given the power to make a wrong into a right. She needed to be accountable for herself. This is how children learn. Tough love sometimes for parents.

As you are in this parent/child relationship together, it is also important for you the parent to learn and take responsibility.

An Aha! Moment

"You cannot control other people's behaviour,
But you can control your responses to it."
—Roberta Cava

My own experience with my young children in taking responsibility for my actions, happened when my children were just six and four. This was one of my biggest 'Aha!' moments in my life. I realize now, had I given in to my first reaction, it would have had a negative impact on my children. Remember that these lessons are not just for kids, they are for us parents too.

One day, the kids were dropped off to my place and the person dropping them off made a derogatory comment about me to the kids.

When the kids entered our house, they told me of this comment and I could tell they wanted to hug me but that if they did, it would be a betrayal to this person, so began the dance of emotions... lean in...lean out. I was so hurt by this ... not so much they said this, but of the behaviour of the kids being torn, it tore my insides up.

I began to cry even though that was the last thing I wanted to do but, I couldn't hold it back. My son was very sensitive and it hurt him to see me cry. He came up to me sitting on the floor in tears, and put his little hand on my shoulder and said, "Mommy, why don't you call that person a bad name too and that will make you feel better."

As you can imagine, the name I wanted to call this person at that moment, was right on the tip of my tongue waiting to be released, waiting ... then my head said, 'wait!' That was the best thing to happen, my head said stop, and I actually did before saying anything. During that moment of stop, thoughts filled my head. I thought, if I did call this person a bad name at this moment, what does that actually accomplish? How will the kids be affected by me doing this? What will that teach my children now and later in life? Is that the message I want to teach them? What good would it do? Think ... what else can I do? How can

I handle this so the kids learn something? Can I turn this around into a positive lesson?

My answer came to me, and I looked at my children and said, "I am not going to call that person a bad name, I really don't think it will make me feel any better, and for sure it won't make you feel good. That person loves you very much and is doing the very best they can, at this moment. I think what we can learn from this is, that it is not very nice to call people names because it hurts people's feelings. Let's promise not to ever call anybody a bad name, let's make sure that we don't make someone feel sad or bad about themselves because, it hurts very badly."

We have the responsibility and power to turn a bad into good in so many situations. What we need to learn as parents is how to stop, unplug from the situation and ask ourselves a few questions. There is no law that says as a parent we need to have all the answers to everything, in an instant. Take a moment to breathe and think, so you can respond and not react.

Responsibility Rewards

"With great power
Comes great responsibility."
—Benjamin Parker

There were also times I gave my children the benefit of the doubt. I would grant them permission to do things they shouldn't do, and I also had a theory about it. This would not apply for every child nor recommended for every child. This is where communication and understanding of your child is so very important, so that you can make decisions, knowing your child will be responsible and you can trust them.

When my kids entered high school, I looked back at when I was in high school. I remembered skipping classes; I was not perfect. I also knew that my children would likely participate in taking off a few classes here and there. Because they had shown me they were responsible, I talked to them about skipping classes. I did share with them, that I remembered taking the odd one off now and then. I told them they are responsible now for their choices. I said since they were now responsible and old enough to operate a motor vehicle, they should also be able to carry the responsibility of going to class or not.

I told them my ask from them was, if they should decide to miss a class they must call me and let me know where they would be, and who they would be with. I said that life is full of surprises, and if something happened in the moment they decided to skip school, I needed to know where they were and how to get hold of them in an emergency. They also agreed to the responsibility to complete the work they missed, on time, without asking for an extension from their teacher. They agreed.

> *"Few things help an individual more than to place responsibility upon him and to let him know that you trust him."* —Booker T. Washington

As it turned out, neither of my children took advantage of this often. When you give responsibility to a young adult, such as someone in high school, they can take it seriously. Also, giving them the responsibility I believe, took away the fun of sneaking off without thought.

On the occasions they did skip class, I would get a call from them and they would tell me where they were going and who they were with. I would also ask if any other parent was aware, and their answer was no, no other parent is getting a call. At least if something did happen to someone, I knew where they were and there is a little more safely in that. Also, after high school and when they are off to college or university, no one really cares if you show up or not, so this was a way of teaching them to be responsible for themselves.

Know your child, and what they are capable of, and make your rules accordingly.

CHILDREN AND MONEY

"Don't educate your children to be Rich.
Educate them to be Happy,
So they know the Value of Things
Not the Price."
—Victor Hugo

Whether you come from a high earning job or are budgeting to the last penny, this subject is an important one. Have you asked yourself what you want to teach your children about money, or have you not thought about it at all? It really is a subject that is too important to ignore.

In my adult life, I have experienced two worlds, living in a 900 square foot home, with no heat except for the wood that I chopped myself and burned in a little wood stove to heat the entire home to... living in a 7000 square foot home with an infinity pool, hot tub, theatre and gym. From my experience of living in both places, I learned that it doesn't matter the size of the box you live in, or the comforts that go with it. What does matter is what goes on inside the box, with the people living in it.

For those that have the money for luxuries, that is fantastic. It is still time for you to consider what you will teach your children about money. Many duo working couples are working so hard to provide these luxuries for their children because, they truly believe the 'stuff' will make up for the time spent absent and apart. In most cases, it doesn't.

> *"For I don't care too much for money, -for money can't buy me love."* —The Beatles

Children enjoy the things they have however, in the end, these 'things' are simply unable to satisfy the very basic need of love. We may 'love' our new toy but, it is only for a moment until something better catches our eye, and this is a message for adults and children alike. This new 'toy' is great for a time but, it simply cannot love us in return. Think about that for just a minute, when you have all the things you say you love, and you still feel a need for something more... what's really missing? Why do we love *things* that simply cannot love us in return? The new toy cannot wrap arms around you to comfort you when you are down, it cannot solve your inner problems or give you advise or even listen or care about who you are. We run from toy to toy (both adults and children) and the toys become bigger and better, and still leave us feeling empty, still looking for what we will never find in a 'thing.'

As adults, we see and hear stories of people that have all the money they could want, and yet they are still not happy... why?

There simply is no substitute for Love. It is not the 'things' that give us meaning and happiness... it is our self, inside that decides our happiness. When you buy a new car, it is so exciting for the first possibly, three months. After that, the excitement has worn off and we are looking at the next 'thing' we can acquire to excite us. Wonder what the world would be like if we worked as hard on our inner self, as we do setting out to get the next latest and greatest.

The pursuit of things is an empty journey, and if 'things' are given to our children regularly without thought, it can create children with an overboard sense of entitlement. When your children venture out into the world and they have always gotten what they wanted, then struggle to find in real life they cannot always have what they want, for some, this is a difficult transition. Unless of course, the parents provide for their children throughout their lifetime. Have you included this in your own financial plan?

> *"Too many people spend money they haven't earned, to buy things they don't want, to impress people they don't like."* —Will Smith

Our society has become obsessed with the power of money, and what things it can get you. For the mainstream family, many suffer from exorbitant debt and the household income cannot sustain the wants, yet we cannot stop our want for things. So many don't care about the debt or interest costs, only how much a month will it be? Adults will choose the weight of money stress in order to be able to show the world their financial success... the irony is that you are not successful, if you have more debt than you can handle. Instead of success... you have a mess.

A circle of not getting anywhere financially begins. The parent wants things like big screen televisions, vacations, cars, boats, trailers and then the kids want items like Xbox, computers, iPhones, and iPads. The parents pursue their own goals for materialism, and tell the child how dare they have such expensive wants.

This is not really the child's fault, the child is learning from their parents... so parents, this topic is for *you!* Look at what you are demonstrating regarding money... what are you teaching your child by your behaviour with money? If parents cannot control their wants and desires financially, what are our children going to learn to do?

——— Excessive Debt = Excessive Stress ———

"Debt creates stress,
Stress creates behaviours
That don't lead to happiness."
—Seth Godin

Debt causes stress, stress is passed on to others in your family. You may think it is your own issue but, it is not. Your frustration with your debt comes out on all those around you and everyone suffers, it is not just about *you.*

Learning how to manage your financial position is vital, and in this day and age, so important. Retailers make it so easy to spend our money without thought. These days you don't even have to leave your home to buy virtually anything your heart desires.

Society has changed so much in the last few decades. I can remember a time when stores were open Monday to Saturday, 9am to 5pm. No Sunday or holiday shopping, no evening shopping, as that was meant for family time. You couldn't even write a cheque dated on a Sunday, it wasn't valid. Now, shopping and spending is available 24/7. It is no wonder our society is so far in debt, and family time is only regarded for special occasions, instead of everyday.

I have worked in the financial industry for much of my life, and I have been shocked by what I see. Credit bureaus with ultra high debt load that leads to excessive late payments, write offs, collections, judgements and bankruptcy. Children watch parents at the store hand over a plastic card and believe they can have anything they want, just hand over a plastic card and... it's yours! That is all the child sees.

I am not opposed to getting things that you want. I agree, it is very fun and even more fun when it is affordable. Are you the type that goes on a vacation and then pays for it after or, are you the type that saves for a vacation and comes home with no bills? One way will lead you down a financial disaster path, and the other will give you enjoyment... make sense?

> *"Bad debt is sacrificing your future day needs for your present day desires."* —Suze Orman

Immediate gratification comes with a price, and usually it is more than we can afford. I am not a financial expert however, it really does make more sense to open a few accounts online and label them with, 'home reno's,' 'vacation,' or, 'television' and put a little away from each payday, and then use these funds for your dreams. Determine a contract with yourself, if there is money in the vacation account, then you can spend that and have a great vacation. If there is money in the home reno account, have fun with your reno's. If it is not in the account, you wait until it is.

Financing to have things immediately is not always the best plan. This is where discipline comes in, and why it is so important to teach this to your children. Just as in the beginning of this book, about passing on your inner issues to your children to deal with, when they already have their own issues… if you continue to spend money you don't have, and teach your children to do the same, they will later pass their money issues back on to *you* to help them get out of debt, and it wasn't your debt to begin with. Do you see the cycle?

— Guide Children to a Good Credit Score —

"Your credit rating isn't an indication that you have money,
It's an indication that you have debt!"
—Dave Ramsey

What can we teach our children about the management of money, and how do we do this? First, we need to understand what our children learn from our behaviour. Your children don't see the bill at the end of the month, asking you to take money from your account, and give it to the card issuer. Children need to see and learn how this works.

Take an evening with your children and teach them. You don't have to give them your reality of income and debt, you can use examples in simple terms and amounts that are easy for them to understand, and invite them to see what takes place in paying off that 'plastic card.' This is an important lesson, regardless of your own financial wealth. Your children still need to learn how to manage money. Teach them the importance of what a credit rating is and that if you don't pay, you can lose the ability and privilege to use credit cards again, or lose the ability to buy that new car or home in their future.

As an example, when my kids were young and at the age where they started asking for twenty dollars to do something with their friends, then another fifty dollars to get a new pair of jeans or ten dollars for pocket money, these can add up fast even though they don't seem like overly large amounts individually. When this began to happen, I knew this was the time to teach them about money.

There is a big difference between 'needs' and 'wants.' Begin by establishing the difference between these words. A 'need' is something that we must have like a tooth brush, good food, a warm jacket, things that are a must to our sustainability. A 'want' is something that we desire but, could easily live without it. Our money must be applied to needs and wants in a controllable way.

— Make a Money Plan With Your Child —

"If you couldn't pass on any of your
financial wealth to your children,
But only a set of principles,
What would they be?"
—Tony Robbins

I took my kids to a bank to meet an account manager. I asked that each of my children open an account and have a bank card that was their own. Both their father and I were also named as account holder with our children, as this way we could keep track online as to what they were spending their money on, and we still had some control. Their father and I chose an amount of money to deposit into their account on the first day of each month. You can determine your own amount based on your personal affordability. This can take the form of an allowance, rather than giving the child the money directly, you can deposit it into this account.

The kids were then told that on the first day of each month, they would have a certain amount of money in their account. Once we explained the difference between wants and needs, we told them they were in control of their money. They understood this money was for all their spending needs including going out with friends, movie tickets, new shoes or new clothes, and if they preferred a different shampoo than the rest of the family, and wanted another brand, they could use their own money.

There were also certain rules that went along with this money. The biggest rule was, there would be no more money given to them for anything. If they wanted a new pair of jeans that totalled the entire allowance, they would not be able to go out with their friends for the rest of the month, until the next month when the money was deposited. They were also told they didn't have to spend the money, they could choose to save it and grow the amount they had, to put it into a larger future purchase. The choice was theirs to make.

For the first few months, I monitored what they were spending it on. My daughter always spent all of her money, and much of it went to Hollywood magazines. Not something I thought was a particular good spend however, this was for the purpose of a lesson and I did not interfere. Then, one time she spent most of her money on a new top and didn't have enough to go out with friends. It was a lesson learned. The next time she went shopping, she realized that she could get four tops for the price of one by shopping at a different store. Lesson was beginning to sink in!

My son was always a saver. He would save all his birthday money and anything he earned by doing small jobs. When he turned sixteen, he had enough saved to pay for half of his first car. Eventually my daughter learned the value of wants and needs and how to manage her money, and started saving too. By saving, she used her money to also buy a car. Years later, she sold the car, worked two jobs, saved the majority of her paycheques, and was able to move across the country to attend University. This was the money she used as her living expense instead of asking her parents for money to live on.

They learned the value of money. They learned the difference between wants and needs and how to control their own spending. They became responsible with money. Since that day of setting up the accounts, they have never asked for money for anything. They developed pride in themselves for being able to manage their own choices and finances.

———— Don't Loose the Lesson! ————

"You learn lessons.
A lot of them the hard way."
—Taylor Swift

It is imperative to add, as much as you feel like it wouldn't be that big of a deal to top them up each month if they went over their budget, it will defeat the purpose entirely. They must manage on their own, by their own choices, to learn these lessons. If they are upset because they don't have enough money to go out with friends and end up staying home instead, let them be angry about it. The lesson is learned when they feel uncomfortable, and they begin to understand their responsibility with money. This is their lesson to learn, and it is the parents lesson in discipline for both the child and yourself.

By doing this you are setting them up for a better future. You are empowering them to think and make their own decisions, and living with the consequences before they get into adult life, and a financial disaster.

VALUES AND VALUE OF SELF

"Here are the values that I stand for: honesty, equality,
kindness, compassion, treating people the way you want
to be treated and helping those in need.
To me, those are traditional values."
—Ellen DeGeneres

We hear a lot about teaching our children values. How many parents really do teach this, at a young age? Do many of you wait until a situation arises and then try to teach or, simply just let life flow and deal with it when it comes up?

I am surprised at the number of people that really don't do any teaching on this, and just wait for things to happen and then try to have their children learn and understand the values of your family.

Let's look closely at what values are. They are personal choices on a foundation of who we are, and what we do. They are the train tracks so to speak, that lead in the right direction, a true north. From time to time we all de-rail and fall off the tracks. Our foundational values are what puts us back in alignment again. Think of the foundation of a house. You cannot build walls and put a roof on, if the foundation is not there.

—— Make Your Foundational Values ——
Known to your Children

"It's not hard to make decisions
When you know what your values are."
—Roy Disney

Each family will have different values, and it is important to have your foundational values known to your children. What are the basics that are expected? What grounds you and your family together? If there are no values in place then, there is room for chaos to intrude and that clean-up can be much harder to get under control, than setting family values in the first place.

Each person has their own set of values, many of which are passed down from generation to generation. Some values change over the years just as lives change. I taught my children our values, one of the important ones was, 'being kind and good to others.' As mentioned earlier, we can teach and be unaware the lesson taught, actually registered with our children, until we are shown.

My son grew up with a good grasp on how to treat others, and he became an advocate for those that did not get treated well. When he was in Grade eight, we got called by the principal requesting our attendance at their awards night however, they would not tell us what award he was receiving.

That night, my son received the 'Humanitarian Award' – only one was given out per year by the school. I could not have been more proud of him, and we told him just that. As all awards are important and significant, I explained to my son that this award meant more to me than the academic award, as this spoke about his character and in particular, his character when no one was watching. He did not share our excitement over this award but, politely thanked everyone for coming. Once we were in the car on the way home, he still did not seem overly happy about the award and I couldn't understand why.

I told him again how proud of him I was, and also said that it doesn't seem like he is very excited about it. I thought maybe he was embarrassed for some reason getting this award in front of the school. He looked at me and said, "The award is cool Mom but ... what is a humanitarian anyway?"

I smiled and said, "You just made it ten times better because, you don't even know what you did or what it's about." I explained that because he took the time to work with the kids that needed a little extra help, and offered them to sit in your chair, and just general helping with their needs, the school was recognizing him for this.

He then said, "But Mom, wouldn't anyone do this?'

"Apparently not, Son," I said.

See, he had been taught that taking care of others and helping when he was able to help, was just a way of life, not something to do once in a while. Teach your child not to be a victim, but to have power to do good things for others. This behaviour carried on well up until he graduated. He always helped those who were victimized, and would take the time to try and build their spirit, and their own sense of self. He had the power and he gave it to other children needing it. The interesting part is that he did this freely, without looking for acknowledgement, without a big ego, it was just part of his heart. As I wrote earlier, teach your child that they are not better than others or too good to help someone else.

> *"Family values stand up to injustice and power outside the household."* —Ralph Nader

Values lay out the foundation to one's life. These are important and really no child should be sent off to school without a clear understanding of the family values. Help to guide your child through the first years. Be clear about your explanation and be age appropriate. As your child gets older, you can revisit this subject and adapt the meanings, and add to the values list, so they are always relevant.

Value of Self

> *"Self-worth comes from within,*
> *You cannot give it to someone*
> *And you can't expect others*
> *To give it to you."*
> —Anonymous

Another part of Values is not just having words to live by, the other part is Value of Self. This is one of the most important things we can build and cultivate in our child's life. This is part of shaping their character, and starting young can carry them through their life on a much easier path.

A child who grows up with strong self-value can make much better life choices, has a bigger opportunity in the workforce, and there is a significantly less chance of a child getting involved in drug abuse, alcohol abuse and even sex abuse. These are all great reasons to focus on our children's emotional health, and not leave it up to life's circumstances to teach them.

Value of Self also encompasses pride, which is a high opinion of one's self, dignity, self-respect and with that said, we also need to teach our children about what it means to have an inflated ego, going too far with thinking they are better than everyone.

When my daughter was about eight years old she would spend all her money on Hollywood magazines and pages were ripped out and stuck on her bedroom walls, so many you didn't know what colour the walls were. At first, I didn't think too much of it as it was just something she liked to do. After a while, I looked at the stack of leftover magazines on the floor, and picked them up to look through them. My fear at the time was that at this pivotal age, she was looking at pictures of perfect people. I was concerned, as I did not want my daughter thinking or believing that she needed to live up to this kind of expectation.

I wasn't sure how to handle this and needed to do something more than just tell her myself, that this wasn't a realistic view of what to expect from herself; to live up to these people who appeared perfect in the magazines. I knew my daughter loved music and lyrics so, I found a song by India Arie. The name of this song is called 'Video' and if you should go through something similar with your daughter, I highly recommend listening to the lyrics and sharing them. It was exactly the message that I wanted my daughter to hear, as it is about owning completely all that you are.

"When I look in the mirror and the only one there is me
Every freckle on my face is where it's supposed to be
And I know my creator didn't make no mistakes on me
My feet, my thighs, my lips, my eyes, I'm loving what I see"
—India Arie, *Video*

My daughter and I listened to these lyrics and I think because the message came from music, and not just myself, it helped her to believe in it. It didn't take long before she found a new hobby, and she tossed the magazines in the garbage. From then on, we had many conversations about loving yourself unconditionally.

—— Five Words: I am Proud of You! ——

"Have you ever looked at your kids
And had your heart filled with so much Love and pride
that it brought tears to your eyes?
I have, and it's amazing."
—Unknown

Many have grown up not ever hearing the words 'I am proud of you' from their parents, and long to. This is not a reward, but a genuine feeling that is expressed from person to person. It is personal.

Think to yourself, how do you feel internally when someone says they are proud of you or, of something you have accomplished, and the words are said very genuinely. Your body seems to react and stands tall, you feel good about yourself, your self-esteem rises, your confidence grows and the next time you go to do something, you want to do your best because that feeling inspired you. How about we have our children feel like they can accomplish what they set their mind to, how about we empower them to do their best, and acknowledge it with our words. It is not whether you win or lose, only that you did your best.

There is a fine line between pride and ego. We want a recipe of just enough pride but, not too much that it turns into ego.

This is also why we need to teach our kids how to handle failure. Ego is about the self, and is conceit. It is self-centred: I, Me, Myself. Explain the meaning of both these words with your children so they have a good understanding of what to be, and what not to be.

——— Help Your Children Find Pride ——— at Home and Within

"Take care of how you speak to yourself
Because...
You are listening."
—Lisa Hayes

The other reason pride is so valuable if taught properly, is it can help your children not to look for pride from outside the home, and in the streets. We all need to be and feel proud of ourselves, it is a motivator. If it is not given in the proper way at home, children will venture out in the world and look for a way to have others tell them they are proud of them. Seeking this from outside can lead your child into the wrong company and they find they are receiving a false pride, someone telling them they are proud of them, to use that against them later.

Many times, when my children did something to be proud of, I would tell them, "Wow, I am so very proud of you for ..." I would also then ask, "Are you proud of you?" By doing this they knew how to be proud of themselves, without needing acknowledgement from others. They were able to empower themselves in this way.

APPRECIATION AND GRATITUDE

*"As we express our gratitude, we must never forget that the
highest appreciation
Is not to utter words, but to live my them."*
—John F. Kennedy

Appreciation; to value justly... and Gratitude; means to be thankful. Two words with such big meaning.

When my kids were seven and nine, a moment presented itself to me to teach my kids the meaning of appreciation. It was a hard lesson but, one that proved much later in years, as a great lesson. It was Christmas, and at the time I was living paycheque to paycheque, which meant that extras for the kids' entertainment was not available easily through the year. I saved my money that particular year so I could lavish my children at Christmas, and found it didn't go as planned.

I bought the kids many gifts, small ones but many, and the tree was full. I was excited and proud of all I had accomplished on such little means. Christmas morning came, and the gifts were handed out and there were yelps of joy from the kids. Just what I was hoping for. I kept watching them and realized that aside from the single yelp, the gift was tossed aside and they were on to the next gift to unwrap. Wrapping paper was strewn all over the floor, along with the gift they had opened. As I watched, horror began to creep inside of me. Disappointment filled my being.

Once the last gift was unwrapped, paper tossed and gifts put to the side, the kids looked at me with wide excited eyes and said, "Is there anything else?" I was mortified. I looked at them stunned and said, "Can you tell me what all of the presents were that you just unwrapped?" They both came back with a hesitation and then started to guess. They really had not registered what they had received, only that there were presents to unwrap. Neither stopped to really look at the gift, and appreciate it. My hard work and anticipation of their thrill was dissolved.

> *"Feeling gratitude and not expressing it is like wrapping a present and not giving it."*
> —William Arthur Ward

I thought for a moment and then asked, "Can you tell me what you got for Christmas two years ago?" Neither had an answer, just a blank look. Then I asked what a family member did two years ago at Christmas, and they quickly started laughing at the time that their relative did something hilarious. Funny, I thought, and it proves my theory.

The most important thing about Christmas was not the wrapping paper and material gifts. The real joy and memories were created by family and time together. I then looked at my kids and said, "There are no more gifts to unwrap and, there will be no more Christmas gifts in the future." My kids looked at me blankly, surely thinking I couldn't possibly be serious. I was very serious.

I explained that Mommy didn't make a lot of money and I had saved all year, I thought all year about what gifts would make them happy and then set out to numerous stores, taking much of my time, just to get the right gift. Then I had to hide the gift and when it was time, wrap it special, and the whole time I was thinking how proud I was and how happy you would be, how much you would appreciate it. Within under three minutes of unwrapping the gift, it was already forgotten.

I began to teach them appreciation. I told them that it is not just when Mom buys you a gift but, when anyone gives them something, even a card, you must take the time to appreciate everything about that gift, and then say thank you. I asked them to consider how they would feel if they spent a month drawing me the perfect picture, one that you were incredibly proud of to present to me. What if I just took a quick look and tossed it on the floor and said, "What else is there?" How would they feel? They both said they would be hurt and upset. Then they began to understand the concept of appreciation.

──────── Appreciation vs. Entitlement ────────

"Be thankful for what you have;
You'll end up having more.
If you concentrate on what you don't have,
You will never, ever have enough."
—Oprah Winfrey

The last thing we need to do is raise children to have an attitude of entitlement. This is what happens if we do not teach them how to appreciate things and gestures. This world does not revolve around anyone… we are in this together to help each other. We need to be grateful, on a daily basis for what we already have, and not keep longing for what we don't have.

Being grateful is something that must be taught, not just expected of our children. Again, how can they know the meaning of the words appreciate and grateful unless we take a moment to teach them, and give them examples of the behaviour that goes with them. Fill your children on the inside, and they won't want the stuff on the outside.

From then on, we only gave a gift of a memory or something that was homemade. If there were no gifts at all, that was absolutely acceptable too, as from then on, Christmas was about the meeting of family, sharing laughter and food. We all enjoyed Christmas more and not less although you would think the opposite. Years later, my kids saw me in the kitchen with a tea towel pinned to my waist. My daughter asked what on earth I was wearing, and I told her it was my apron, and we laughed. Christmas came and my kids gave me a new apron, not just any apron, one that was homemade.

It was a full apron, on plain fabric. My kids bought fabric paint and on the top wrote, 'Remember that time …'. Then they wrote little things about their childhood. My daughter wrote about my son, and my son wrote about my daughter. Some notes were hilarious, some made me cry and some made me do both, laugh and cry! They included their hand print, and at the bottom wrote, 'And we never stopped loving you …'. This is the true meaning of a gift. I still am amazed at how this came about, as at the time my son and daughter were living on opposite sides of Canada. They had to come up with the idea, and then managed to get together to accomplish this, and the effort warms my heart. No, I do not use the apron, I just cannot spill something on this precious work of art!

The Joys of Volunteering

"Alone we can do so little;
Together we can do so much."
—Helen Keller

One of the best ways to help your child feel appreciation and gratitude is to have them volunteer their time for someone or, groups less fortunate than themselves. It can be amazing what doors open for those that do, and what a great feeling it is inside to help someone. It also teaches your child to see a world outside of themselves.

Voluntarism is something that I have done my entire life, and I do not feel complete unless I am doing… something. One of the first times my children came with me to volunteer, they really didn't fully understand what they were doing, or more of why they were doing it. I took them with me to the Heart and Stroke Foundation to help prepare goodie bags for the children running for the cause. As we were not runners, this was our way to contribute. It was a simple task in which we filled little bags with goodies for the children that were participating in the run. When we left, I sat with the kids and we talked about what they had just done.

I told them that just by doing what they did today, it helps to raise money for research for people who are suffering with heart problems, and that in a roundabout way, when everything comes together from filling goodie bags, to the runners, to the gathering of donations, to the research, they are a part of saving someone's life, even just one person. I asked how they felt now knowing this … they were amazed and felt wonderful and wanted to do this again. The ironic thing about this was, years later, my daughter developed a problem with her heart that required surgery. We talked about the help they had given years ago to the cause, and now she was a recipient of all the good work that volunteers do.

> *"The best way to find yourself is to lose yourself in the service of others."* —Ghandi

We had several opportunities to do many things like this over their young years and teen years. A few times I dressed up as a mascot for a cause and had them join me because, I could not see out of the costume and I needed someone to hold my arm and guide me. This was not the greatest thing for my children to do in a busy mall when their friends are shopping, and they are holding on to a mascot that is your mom, but they learned by the experience and the importance of it.

As my children and I volunteered together, it grew to be a part of my children's life.

> *"Give. Even when you know you can get nothing back."* —Yasmin Mogahed

One night my son called to tell me that he didn't feel he had accomplished much that day. He said before he went to bed he cleaned his closet and put things he was no longer wearing into a knapsack, and went to town. He approached the homeless, and asked if they were warm enough and when they said no, he pulled out socks or a sweater, shared cookies with them, and took the time to chat with them. He said to me, "They are really nice people, Mom!" He did this on his own, without coaching or without expectation of anything in return.

We can teach our children to have an open heart, to be part of the solution and have compassion for others. If we can be a good role model as parents, and show them how to give of themselves, they will take it on without even thinking about it.

I have volunteered most of my life, several times for local organizations including facilitating two parenting programs, one for parents of teens wanting a better relationship with their teenage children, and another for single parents. I have also travelled several times to Romania, to work in an orphanage and the poor gypsy villages. When I came home, I would share with my kids about my lessons and experiences.

In 2010, I travelled to the Dominican Republic to work in Haitian villages. I fell in love with a little girl who was just six, being bullied severely and was not permitted to go to school or to church, all because she had a deformity on her face that the village thought may have been contagious. I took her under my wing, and I was able to get her the medical attention she needed and supply her with food and school supplies. She is now fourteen and top of her class, and all the children in the village that bullied her, are now her best friends. A lesson in forgiveness for sure! I have been there once or twice a year since then, to see how she is and I also help and assist my dear friend, Karen Lee Conquergood* in delivering food to several villages, some suffering from HIV/AIDs and some from abject poverty. My daughter has accompanied me twice, and has also made some great relationships with some of the girls in the village, and she calls my little girl there, her sister. She said to me, "Mom, I have seen all your photos and heard all your stories but, to be here is completely different."

> **"The intelligent way to be selfish is to work for the welfare of others."** —Dalai Lama

When children become a part of something bigger than themselves, they have a better understanding of the world around them, and are able to see the world, and not just themselves in it.

* Karen Lee Conquergood, further information is available under 'Suggested Further Reading'

FUN, LAUGHTER AND MEMORIES

"The most wasted of all days is one without laughter."
—e.e. cummings

While we are organizing, cleaning, teaching, disciplining and doing everything else in life we need to do for our children, please remember to have fun and laugh with your children. It costs nothing and is very bonding. My kids expressed their sense of humour every day and at times they get each other going, and to watch the way they feed off each other and perform is something. There were not many days that I wasn't caught up in an outrageous belly laugh because of them.

Sometimes when things are stressful, the only option is to laugh about it. If it is something that won't matter five years from now, if it is something that is not harmful to your children or others but, still carries stress ... laugh about it. Sometimes minimizing things that we cannot control, laughing is a helpful way to cope.

Break out of the parental box and do things from time to time that are unpredictable. The memories of this will last a lifetime. One night for dinner I made Kraft dinner, not something we had often but, it was chosen this night on purpose. I put their dinner plates on the table and said I wanted them to finish all their dinner. As I turned to walk away my son said, "But Mom, we don't have a fork." I smiled and said, "I know, and you will not be getting one, and you are not allowed to use your hands. Figure it out!" Well, they dove in face first and ate their dinner between laughter! It was everywhere, on the floor, on the table and all over their faces! The only harm was a little mess that was easy to clean up. I truly don't even remember cleaning up, only the laughter!

> *"Laughter is, and will always be the best form of therapy."* —Unknown

Many years later, when my kids were grown I had them over to carve pumpkins for Halloween. We each had a pumpkin to carve, and when we made the lids and cleaned out all the stuff on the inside, there was a mound of insides on the table. While they were starting to do the face of the pumpkin, I picked up the insides with my hands, and started tossing it at my kids! Well, this was worse than a food fight! It was all over the floor, the walls, in our hair and on the blinds, on the windows, our clothes, everywhere! We all laughed so hard and partly because, I was the one to start it all.

—— Release Your Inner Child – Have Fun! ——

"That is the real trouble with the world,
Too many people grow up."
—Walt Disney

Take time to have fun, messes are easy. It doesn't have to cost a lot and doing things out of the ordinary, creates moments to remember. I also used to tie a string on a plastic grocery bag and tell them to pretend it was a kite, and run around the cul-de-sac, they did, and they still remember and laugh about it.

As mentioned in the beginning of the book, I do not recall many memories as a child and because of this, I wanted my children to have a box full of memories that would make them laugh and smile for the rest of their life. One day my son, at about the age of nine, was invited to spend a weekend with a friend and their family at a cabin. My son looked at me and said, "I don't really want to go but, I guess I will just go and make a memory."

I would get out in the summer evenings and play basketball with my son or, at times we would play road hockey. He would have a great time putting all the padding on me, and putting me in net to take shots on me … we had so much fun until, he grew and his shots were harder. Then we switched, I put him in net, and took shots on him!

When my kids were growing up I kept everything from their childhood. When I say everything, I mean *everything!* From lost teeth to braces, from notes they wrote to each other to special cards, from their first pair of shoes to their last toy they played with, and everything in between. Each of my children had their own box. When they were about nineteen and twenty-one, I wrapped these up and gave them to them at Christmas. We had so much fun going through the boxes, named memory boxes by the kids, and they could not believe I had kept so much from their childhood. What great memories, and what a great bonding time for us all.

> *"To be in your child's memories tomorrow, you have to be in their lives today."*
> —Barbara Johnson

I give you permission to release your inner child and get down and join your children in fun times. Be goofy, be spontaneous, and be happy!!

TO CONCLUDE AND SUM IT ALL UP

"It is not what you do for your children,
But what you have taught them to do for themselves
That will make them successful human beings."
—Ann Landers

It is interesting how we go to classes to learn how to give birth. We learn how to breathe between contractions and what is to be expected and yet, there is nothing to help us along with raising the children, which is the most important thing we can do.

- Treat your children how you would want to be treated. Teach them how to treat you.
- If you would like to be heard, hear them.
- If you want to be treated with respect, treat them with respect.
- If you want to be understood, understand them.
- If you don't want your child to be a bully, don't bully them.
- Always keep the mirror on yourself, so you can see what a child sees in you.

We are all busy, good parenting is a choice first to be one. Remember every day what a gift they are, and that what you do each day will have an effect and impact on your child, good or bad. You reap what you sew.

Be present when your child needs you. You cannot get that time back, once it passes, it is gone. It would be great if we could schedule talk time for once a week to fit our busy life but, that is just not reality. It would be like making an appointment with your mechanic because of a rattle, and when you show up for your appointment, the rattle is not there anymore.

Be consistent, when you say no, explain why, and stick to it. When they do something good, reward them with your time and acknowledgement for the good deed, consistently. Children are in basic training. Build the trust and openness, this is worth its weight in gold.

If you make a mistake as a parent, apologize to your children. What they see you do, they will also do. It is not enough to just say sorry, explain why you are sorry so your children will do the same.

Please don't project to your child that you are perfect because, none of us are. We learn how to parent every day, with every experience. If your child views you as perfect, they will believe they also need to be perfect and that is just not possible to live up to. Tell your child some of your faults so they view you as being like them, and they will be less afraid to come to you with a problem, because they know you have them too.

Love your child unconditionally. Let them know that nothing they do or say will ever make you stop loving them. Make them feel secure in this.

Know that it is never too late to start these behaviours. If your child is a little older and is acting out, usually it is because they are lacking understanding, a safe place to vent, or are feeling neglected. Sometimes they will not be able to communicate what is bothering them because, they don't understand it themselves. Cut them some slack with your expectations, and let them show you who they are.

Stop and think before reacting to a situation. Ask yourself, how can I respond in a way that is loving, caring, and will teach my child a life lesson. Many of these situations that you deal with, your child will have a life lesson that can be taught. If you cannot come up with anything, you can give yourself permission to tell your child, "I am not sure how to respond to this at the moment, I need a little time to think about this and we will talk about this in a little while." That can save you from giving your child emotional damage, and stop you from saying something you might regret.

Don't assume that your child understands things the way you do. Take time to explain, explain words and their meanings and behaviours. Also, remember that children can pick up on energy we give off. If we are angry or upset and say nothing, don't think you are fooling your child, they will feel it just the same as you can feel from others that something is wrong. The elephant in the room is big enough to feel no matter your age. We need to be responsible as parents for our own feelings, and communicate to our children about them.

If we begin parenting at a place of consciousness when the children are young, your teens will end up in a much better mind space. I have seen parents struggle during the teen years because there was no foundation laid when the kids were young. Do yourself a favour, and your children a favour, and start young. Make your discussions age appropriate, and ask them what their thoughts are, and cultivate good communication.

Empower your children, learn with them and grow with them, you are in this together.

ONE... that is the number of chances you have, to get this as right as possible.

A baby is a baby... ONE time.

An adolescent is and adolescent... ONE time.

A teenager is a teenager... ONE time.

"All kids need is a little help,
A little hope,
And someone that believes in them."
—Magic Johnson

Raising my children has been the most profound,
and amazing journey of my life...
and I hope it will be yours too.

And... breathe again....
You've Got This!!!

SUGGESTED FURTHER READING

For those who want to explore some topics in further detail, you may wish to consult the following:

Cline, F. and Fay, J. (2014). *Parenting with Love and Logic: Teaching Children Responsibility.* (Carol Stream, IL: NavPress)

Faber, A. and Mazlich, E. (2012). *How to Talk So Kids Will Listen & Listen So Kids Will Talk.* (New York: Scribner)

Chapman, Gary (1995). *The Five Love Languages: The Secret to Love that Lasts.* (Chicago, IL: Northfield)

Coloroso, Barbara (1994). *Kids Are Worth It.* (Toronto, Ont: Penguin)

Vannoy, Steven W. (1994). *The 10 Greatest Gifts I Give My Children.* (New York: Fireside)

Zukav, Gary (1989). *The Seat of the Soul.* (New York: Simon & Schuster)

*** For more information about the good work that Karen Lee Conquergood is doing to help the lives of the people in the Dominican Republic or, to make a donation, please visit:

dominicanaid.us

kconquergood@gmail.com

www.ingramcontent.com/pod-product-compliance
Lightning Source LLC
LaVergne TN
LVHW042149020525
810250LV00004B/728